Apache Spark 2.x Cookbook

Cloud-ready recipes to do analytics and data science on
Apache Spark

Rishi Yadav

BIRMINGHAM - MUMBAI

Apache Spark 2.x Cookbook

First published: May 2017

Production reference: 1300517

Published by Packt Publishing Ltd.
Livery Place
35 Livery Street
Birmingham
B3 2PB, UK.
ISBN 978-1-78712-726-5

www.packtpub.com

Credits

Author
Rishi Yadav

Reviewer
Prashant Verma

Commissioning Editor
Amey Varangaonkar

Acquisition Editor
Vinay Argekar

Content Development Editor
Jagruti Babaria

Technical Editor
Dinesh Pawar

Copy Editor
Gladson Monteiro

Project Coordinator
Nidhi Joshi

Proofreader
Safis Editing

Indexer
Pratik Shirodkar

Graphics
Tania Dutta

Production Coordinator
Sharddha Falebhai

About the Author

Rishi Yadav has 19 years of experience in designing and developing enterprise applications. He is an open source software expert and advises American companies on big data and public cloud trends. Rishi was honored as one of Silicon Valley's 40 under 40 in 2014. He earned his bachelor's degree from the prestigious Indian Institute of Technology, Delhi, in 1998.

About 12 years ago, Rishi started InfoObjects, a company that helps data-driven businesses gain new insights into data. InfoObjects combines the power of open source and big data to solve business challenges for its clients and has a special focus on Apache Spark. The company has been on the Inc. 5000 list of the fastest growing companies for 6 years in a row. InfoObjects has also been named the best place to work in the Bay Area in 2014 and 2015.

Rishi is an open source contributor and active blogger.

This book is dedicated to my parents, Ganesh and Bhagwati Yadav; I would not be where I am without their unconditional support, trust, and providing me the freedom to choose a path of my own.
Special thanks go to my life partner, Anjali, for providing immense support and putting up with my long, arduous hours (yet again).
Our 9-year-old son, Vedant, and niece, Kashmira, were the unrelenting force behind keeping me and the book on track.
Big thanks to InfoObjects' CTO and my business partner, Sudhir Jangir, for providing valuable feedback and also contributing with recipes on enterprise security, a topic he is passionate about; to our SVP, Bart Hickenlooper, for taking the charge in leading the company to the next level; to Tanmoy Chowdhury and Neeraj Gupta for their valuable advice; to Yogesh Chandani, Animesh Chauhan, and Katie Nelson for running operations skillfully so that I could focus on this book; and to our internal review team (especially Rakesh Chandran) for ironing out the kinks. I would also like to thank Marcel Izumi for, as always, providing creative visuals. I cannot miss thanking our dog, Sparky, for giving me company on my long nights out. Last but not least, special thanks to our valuable clients, partners, and employees, who have made InfoObjects the best place to work at and, needless to say, an immensely successful organization.

About the Reviewer

Prashant Verma started his IT career in 2011 as a Java developer at Ericsson, working in the telecom domain. After a couple of years of Java EE experience, he moved into the big data domain and has worked on almost all the popular big data technologies, such as Hadoop, Spark, Flume, Mongo, and Cassandra. He has also played with Scala. Currently, he works with QA Infotech as a lead data engineer, working on solving e-learning problems using analytics and machine learning.

Prashant has also been working as a freelance consultant in his spare time.

I want to thank Packt Publishing for giving me the chance to review the book as well as my employer and my family for their patience while I was busy working on this book.

www.PacktPub.com

For support files and downloads related to your book, please visit www.PacktPub.com.

Did you know that Packt offers eBook versions of every book published, with PDF and ePub files available? You can upgrade to the eBook version at www.PacktPub.comand as a print book customer, you are entitled to a discount on the eBook copy. Get in touch with us at service@packtpub.com for more details.

At www.PacktPub.com, you can also read a collection of free technical articles, sign up for a range of free newsletters and receive exclusive discounts and offers on Packt books and eBooks.

https://www.packtpub.com/mapt

Get the most in-demand software skills with Mapt. Mapt gives you full access to all Packt books and video courses, as well as industry-leading tools to help you plan your personal development and advance your career.

Why subscribe?

- Fully searchable across every book published by Packt
- Copy and paste, print, and bookmark content
- On demand and accessible via a web browser

Customer Feedback

Thanks for purchasing this Packt book. At Packt, quality is at the heart of our editorial process. To help us improve, please leave us an honest review on this book's Amazon page at `https://www.amazon.com/dp/1787127265`.

If you'd like to join our team of regular reviewers, you can e-mail us at `customerreviews@packtpub.com`. We award our regular reviewers with free eBooks and videos in exchange for their valuable feedback. Help us be relentless in improving our products!

Table of Contents

Preface

The success of Hadoop as a big data platform raised user expectations, both in terms of solving different analytics challenges and reducing latency. Various tools evolved over time, but when Apache Spark came, it provided a single runtime to address all these challenges. It eliminated the need to combine multiple tools with their own challenges and learning curves. Using memory for persistent storage besides compute, Apache Spark eliminates the need to store intermediate data on disk and increases processing speed up to 100 times. It also provides a single runtime, which addresses various analytics needs, such as machine-learning and real-time streaming, using various libraries.

This book covers the installation and configuration of Apache Spark and building solutions using Spark Core, Spark SQL, Spark Streaming, MLlib, and GraphX libraries.

 For more information on this book's recipes, please visit infoobjects.com/spark-cookbook.

What this book covers

Chapter 1, *Getting Started with Apache Spark*, explains how to install Spark on various environments and cluster managers.

Chapter 2, *Developing Applications with Spark*, talks about developing Spark applications on different IDEs and using different build tools.

Chapter 3, *Spark SQL*, covers how to read and write to various data sources.

Chapter 4, *Working with External Data Sources*, takes you through the Spark SQL module that helps you access the Spark functionality using the SQL interface.

Chapter 5, *Spark Streaming*, explores the Spark Streaming library to analyze data from real-time data sources, such as Kafka.

Chapter 6, *Getting Started with Machine Learning*, covers an introduction to machine learning and basic artifacts, such as vectors and matrices.

Chapter 7, *Supervised Learning with MLlib – Regression*, walks through supervised learning when the outcome variable is continuous.

`Chapter 8`, *Supervised Learning with MLlib – Classification*, discusses supervised learning when the outcome variable is discrete.

`Chapter 9`, *Unsupervised Learning*, covers unsupervised learning algorithms, such as k-means.

`Chapter 10`, *Recommendations Using Collaborative Filtering*, introduces building recommender systems using various techniques, such as ALS.

`Chapter 11`, *Graph Processing Using GraphX and GraphFrames*, talks about various graph processing algorithms using GraphX.

`Chapter 12`, *Optimizations and Performance Tuning*, covers various optimizations on Apache Spark and performance tuning techniques.

What you need for this book

There are two ways to work with the recipes in this book:

- The first is to use Databricks Community Cloud at `https://community.cloud.d atabricks.com`. It is a free notebook provided by Databricks. All the sample data for this book has also been uploaded in the Amazon Web Service S3 bucket, namely `sparkcookbook`.
- The second option is to use InfoObjects Big Data Sandbox, which is a virtual machine built on top of Ubuntu. This software can be downloaded from `http ://www.infoobjects.com`.

Who this book is for

If you are a data engineer, an application developer, or a data scientist who would like to leverage the power of Apache Spark to get better insights from big data, then this is the book for you.

Sections

In this book, you will find several headings that appear frequently (Getting ready, How to do it..., How it works..., There's more..., and See also).

To give clear instructions on how to complete a recipe, we use these sections as follows:

Getting ready

This section tells you what to expect in the recipe, and describes how to set up any software or any preliminary settings required for the recipe.

How to do it...

This section contains the steps required to follow the recipe.

How it works...

This section usually consists of a detailed explanation of what happened in the previous section.

There's more...

This section consists of additional information about the recipe in order to make the reader more knowledgeable about the recipe.

See also

This section provides helpful links to other useful information the recipe.

Conventions

In this book, you will find a number of text styles that distinguish between different kinds of information. Here are some examples of these styles and an explanation of their meaning.

Code words in text, database table names, folder names, filenames, file extensions, pathnames, dummy URLs, user input, and Twitter handles are shown as follows: "Spark expects Java to be installed and the JAVA_HOME environment variable to be set."

A block of code is set as follows:

```
[{ "firstName" : "Bill", "lastName": "Clinton", "age": 70 }
      {"firstName": "Barack","lastName": "Obama", "age": 55}]
```

Any command-line input or output is written as follows:

```
scala> val people = spark.sql("select * from person")
```

New terms and **important** words are shown in bold. Words that you see on the screen, for example, in menus or dialog boxes, appear in the text like this: "Click on **Create cluster** and select the last option in the **Applications** option box."

 Warnings or important notes appear in a box like this.

 Tips and tricks appear like this.

Reader feedback

Feedback from our readers is always welcome. Let us know what you think about this book—what you liked or disliked. Reader feedback is important for us as it helps us develop titles that you will really get the most out of.

To send us general feedback, simply e-mail feedback@packtpub.com, and mention the book's title in the subject of your message.

If there is a topic that you have expertise in and you are interested in either writing or contributing to a book, see our author guide at www.packtpub.com/authors.

Customer support

Now that you are the proud owner of a Packt book, we have a number of things to help you to get the most from your purchase.

Downloading the color images of this book

We also provide you with a PDF file that has color images of the screenshots/diagrams used in this book. The color images will help you better understand the changes in the output. You can download this file from:
https://www.packtpub.com/sites/default/files/downloads/ApacheSpark2xCookbook_Co lorImages.pdf.

Errata

Although we have taken every care to ensure the accuracy of our content, mistakes do happen. If you find a mistake in one of our books—maybe a mistake in the text or the code—we would be grateful if you could report this to us. By doing so, you can save other readers from frustration and help us improve subsequent versions of this book. If you find any errata, please report them by visiting http://www.packtpub.com/submit-errata, selecting your book, clicking on the Errata Submission Form link, and entering the details of your errata. Once your errata are verified, your submission will be accepted and the errata will be uploaded to our website or added to any list of existing errata under the Errata section of that title.

To view the previously submitted errata, go to https://www.packtpub.com/books/content/support and enter the name of the book in the search field. The required information will appear under the *Errata* section.

Piracy

Piracy of copyrighted material on the Internet is an ongoing problem across all media. At Packt, we take the protection of our copyright and licenses very seriously. If you come across any illegal copies of our works in any form on the Internet, please provide us with the location address or website name immediately so that we can pursue a remedy.

Please contact us at copyright@packtpub.com with a link to the suspected pirated material.

We appreciate your help in protecting our authors and our ability to bring you valuable content.

Questions

If you have a problem with any aspect of this book, you can contact us at questions@packtpub.com, and we will do our best to address the problem.

1
Getting Started with Apache Spark

In this chapter, we will set up Spark and configure it. This chapter contains the following recipes:

- Leveraging Databricks Cloud
- Deploying Spark using Amazon EMR
- Installing Spark from binaries
- Building the Spark source code with Maven
- Launching Spark on Amazon EC2
- Deploying Spark on a cluster in standalone mode
- Deploying Spark on a cluster with Mesos
- Deploying Spark on a cluster with YARN
- Understanding SparkContext and SparkSession
- Understanding Resilient Distributed Datasets (RDD)

Introduction

Apache Spark is a general-purpose cluster computing system to process big data workloads. What sets Spark apart from its predecessors, such as **Hadoop MapReduce**, is its speed, ease of use, and sophisticated analytics.

It was originally developed at *AMPLab, UC Berkeley*, in *2009*. It was made open source in 2010 under the BSD license and switched to the Apache 2.0 license in 2013. Toward the later part of 2013, the creators of Spark founded Databricks to focus on Spark's development and future releases.

Databricks offers Spark as a service in the **Amazon Web Services(AWS)** Cloud, called Databricks Cloud. In this book, we are going to maximize the use of AWS as a data storage layer.

Talking about speed, Spark can achieve subsecond latency on big data workloads. To achieve such low latency, Spark makes use of memory for storage. In MapReduce, memory is primarily used for the actual computation. Spark uses memory both to compute and store objects.

Spark also provides a unified runtime connecting to various big data storage sources, such as HDFS, Cassandra, and S3. It also provides a rich set of high-level libraries for different big data compute tasks, such as machine learning, SQL processing, graph processing, and real-time streaming. These libraries make development faster and can be combined in an arbitrary fashion.

Though Spark is written in Scala--and this book only focuses on recipes on Scala--it also supports Java, Python, and R.

Spark is an open source community project, and everyone uses the pure open source Apache distributions for deployments, unlike Hadoop, which has multiple distributions available with vendor enhancements.

The following figure shows the Spark ecosystem:

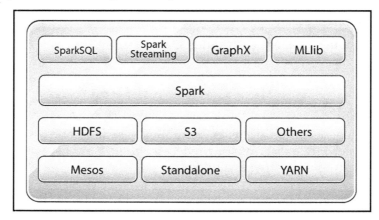

Spark's runtime runs on top of a variety of cluster managers, including **YARN** (Hadoop's compute framework), **Mesos**, and Spark's own cluster manager called **Standalone** mode. Alluxio is a memory-centric distributed file system that enables reliable file sharing at memory speed across cluster frameworks. In short, it is an off-heap storage layer in memory that helps share data across jobs and users. Mesos is a cluster manager, which is evolving into a data center operating system. YARN is Hadoop's compute framework and has a robust resource management feature that Spark can seamlessly use.

Apache Spark, initially devised as a replacement of MapReduce, had a good proportion of workloads running in an on-premises manner. Now, most of the workloads have been moved to public clouds (AWS, Azure, and GCP). In a public cloud, we see two types of applications:

- Outcome-driven applications
- Data transformation pipelines

For outcome-driven applications, where the goal is to derive a predefined signal/outcome from the given data, Databricks Cloud fits the bill perfectly. For traditional data transformation pipelines, Amazon's **Elastic MapReduce** (**EMR**) does a great job.

Leveraging Databricks Cloud

Databricks is the company behind Spark. It has a cloud platform that takes out all of the complexity of deploying Spark and provides you with a ready-to-go environment with notebooks for various languages. Databricks Cloud also has a community edition that provides one node instance with 6 GB of RAM for free. It is a great starting place for developers. The Spark cluster that is created also terminates after 2 hours of sitting idle.

 All the recipes in this book can be run on either the `InfoObjects` Sandbox or Databricks Cloud community edition. The entire data for the recipes in this book has also been ported to a public bucket called `sparkcookbook` on S3. Just put these recipes on the Databricks Cloud community edition, and they will work seamlessly.

How to do it...

1. Go to `https://community.cloud.databricks.com`:

2. Click on **Sign Up** :

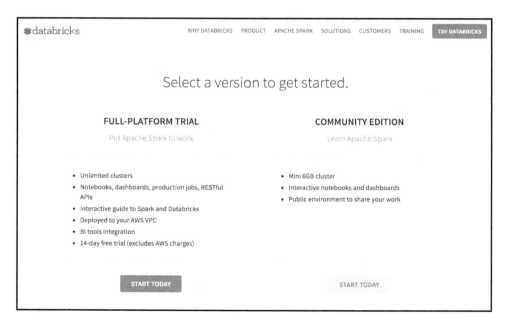

3. Choose **COMMUNITY EDITION** (or full platform):

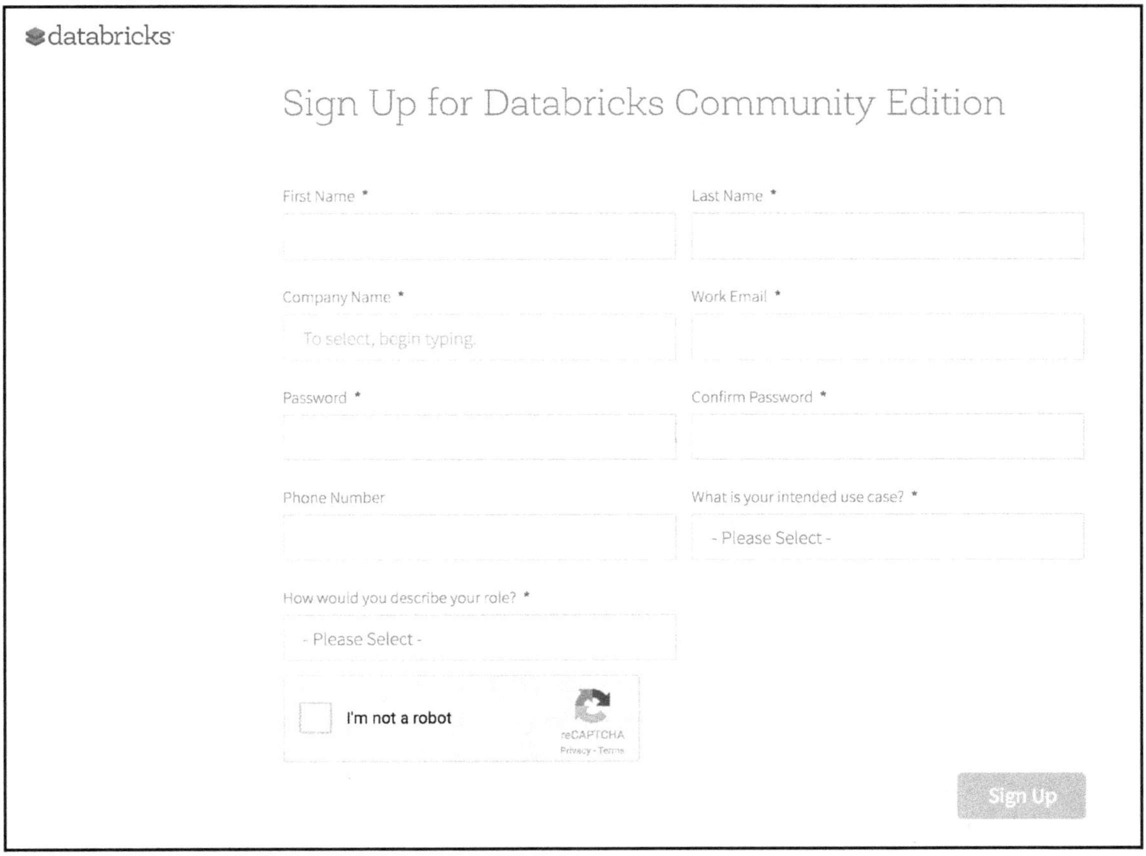

---

databricks

Sign Up for Databricks Community Edition

First Name *

Last Name *

Company Name *

To select, begin typing.

Work Email *

Password *

Confirm Password *

Phone Number

What is your intended use case? *

- Please Select -

How would you describe your role? *

- Please Select -

I'm not a robot

reCAPTCHA
Privacy - Terms

Sign Up

---

4. Fill in the details and you'll be presented with a landing page, as follows:

5. Click on **Clusters**, then **Create Cluster** (showing community edition below it):

6. Enter the cluster name, for example, `myfirstcluster`, and choose **Availability Zone** (more about AZs in the next recipe). Then click on **Create Cluster**:

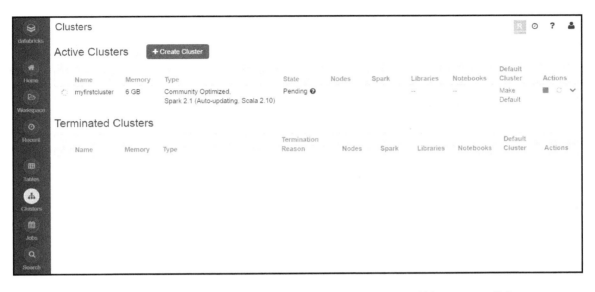

7. Once the cluster is created, the blinking green signal will become solid green, as follows:

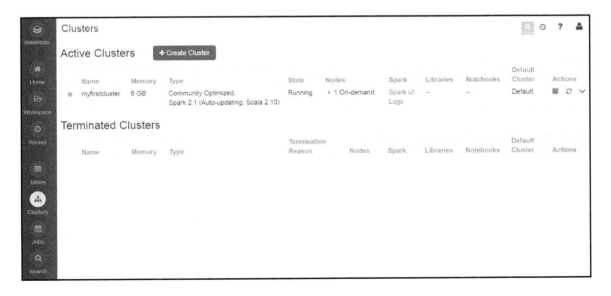

8. Now go to **Home** and click on **Notebook**. Choose an appropriate notebook name, for example, `config`, and choose **Scala** as the language:

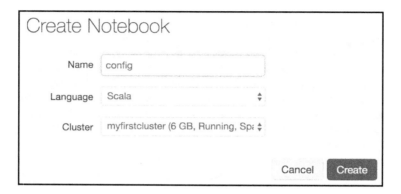

9. Then set the AWS access parameters. There are two access parameters:
   - ACCESS_KEY: This is referred to as `fs.s3n.awsAccessKeyId` in SparkContext's Hadoop configuration.
   - SECRET_KEY: This is referred to as `fs.s3n.awsSecretAccessKey` in SparkContext's Hadoop configuration.

10. Set ACCESS_KEY in the `config` notebook:

```
sc.hadoopConfiguration.set("fs.s3n.awsAccessKeyId", "<replace
    with your key>")
```

11. Set SECRET_KEY in the `config` notebook:

```
sc.hadoopConfiguration.set("fs.s3n.awsSecretAccessKey","
    <replace with your secret key>")
```

12. Load a folder from the `sparkcookbook` bucket (all of the data for the recipes in this book are available in this bucket:

```
val yelpdata =
    spark.read.textFile("s3a://sparkcookbook/yelpdata")
```

13. The problem with the previous approach was that if you were to publish your notebook, your keys would be visible. To avoid the use of this approach, use **Databricks File System (DBFS)**.

DBFS is Databricks Cloud's internal file system. It is a layer above S3, as you can guess. It mounts S3 buckets in a user's workspace as well as caches frequently accessed data on worker nodes.

14. Set the access key in the Scala notebook:

```
val accessKey = "<your access key>"
```

15. Set the secret key in the Scala notebook:

```
val secretKey = "<your secret key>".replace("/", "%2F")
```

16. Set the bucket name in the Scala notebook:

```
val bucket = "sparkcookbook"
```

17. Set the mount name in the Scala notebook:

```
val mount = "cookbook"
```

18. Mount the bucket:

```
dbutils.fs.mount(s"s3a://$accessKey:$secretKey@$bucket",
  s"/mnt/$mount")
```

19. Display the contents of the bucket:

```
display(dbutils.fs.ls(s"/mnt/$mount"))
```

 The rest of the recipes will assume that you would have set up AWS credentials.

How it works...

Let's look at the key concepts in Databricks Cloud.

Cluster

The concept of clusters is self-evident. A cluster contains a master node and one or more slave nodes. These nodes are EC2 nodes, which we are going to learn more about in the next recipe.

Notebook

Notebook is the most powerful feature of Databricks Cloud. You can write your code in Scala/Python/R or a simple SQL notebook. These notebooks cover the whole 9 yards. You can use notebooks to write code like a programmer, use SQL like an analyst, or do visualization like a **Business Intelligence (BI)** expert.

Table

Tables enable Spark to run SQL queries.

Library

Library is the section where you upload the libraries you would like to attach to your notebooks. The beauty is that you do not have to upload libraries manually; you can simply provide the Maven parameters and it would find the library for you and attach it.

Deploying Spark using Amazon EMR

There is a reason why deploying Spark on Amazon EMR is added as one of the first recipes in this edition of the book. The majority of the production deployments of Spark happen on EMR (in fact, the majority, and increasingly so, big data deployments happen on EMR). If you understand this recipe well, you may skip the rest of the recipes in this chapter, unless you are doing an on-premises deployment.

 Since this topic is of paramount importance in the current context, a lot more theory is being provided than what a typical cookbook would have. You can skip the theory section and directly go to the How to do it.. section, but I encourage you not to do so.

What it represents is much bigger than what it looks

What EMR represents is far more than meets the eye. Most of the enterprise workloads are migrating to public clouds at an accelerated pace. Once migrated, these workloads get rearchitected to leverage cloud-based services as opposed to simply using it as **Infrastructure as a Service (IaaS)**. EC2 is an IaaS compute service of AWS, while EMR is the leading **Platform as a Service (PaaS)** service of AWS, with more big data workloads running on EMR than the alternatives combined.

EMR's architecture

Hadoop's core feature is **data locality**, that is, taking compute to where the data is. AWS disrupts this concept by separating storage and compute. AWS has multiple storage options, including the following:

- **Amazon S3**: S3 is general-purpose object storage.
- **Amazon Redshift**: This is a distributed cloud data warehouse.
- **Amazon DynamoDB**: This is a NoSQL database.
- **Amazon Aurora**: This is a cloud-based relational database.

Amazon S3 is the cheapest and most reliable cloud storage available, and this makes it the first choice, unless there is a compelling reason not to do so. EMR also supports attaching **elastic block storage (EBS)** volumes to compute instances (EC2) in order to provide a lower latency option.

Which option to choose depends upon what type of cluster is being created. There are two types of clusters:

- **Persistent cluster**: It runs 24 x 7. Here, there is a continuous analysis of data for use cases such as fraud detection in the financial industry or clickstream analytics in ad tech. For these purposes, HDFS mounted on EBS is a good choice.
- **Transient cluster**: Here, workloads are run inconsistently, for example, genome sequencing or holiday surge in retail. In this case, the cluster is only spawned when needed, making **Elastic Map Reduce File System (EMRFS)** based on S3 a better choice.

How to do it...

1. Log in to `https://aws.amazon.com` with your credentials.
2. Click on **Services** and select/search for EMR:

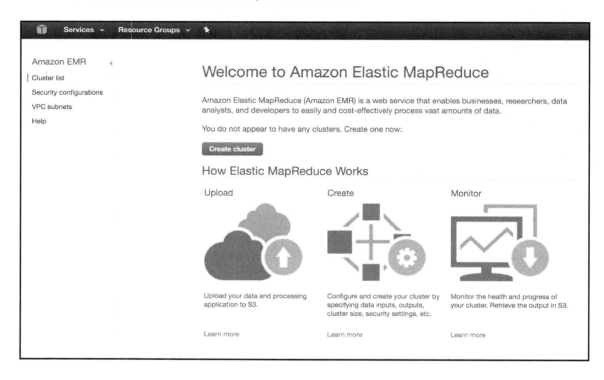

3. Click on **Create cluster** and select the last option in the **Applications** option box:

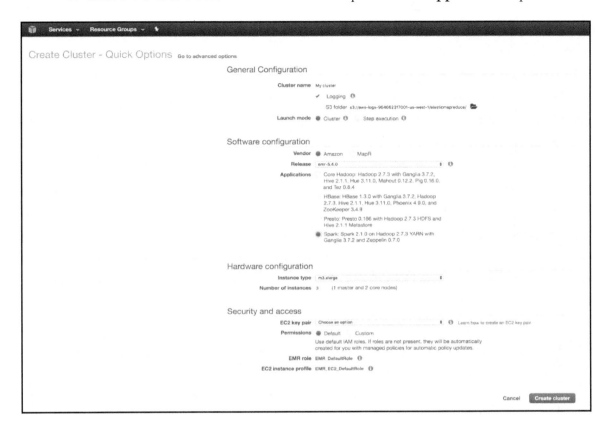

4. Click on **Create Cluster** and the cluster will start as follows:

5. Once the cluster is created with the given configuration, the **My Cluster** status will change to **Waiting**, as shown in the following screenshot:

6. Now add a step to select the JAR file; it takes the input file from the S3 location and produces the output file and stores it in the desired S3 bucket:

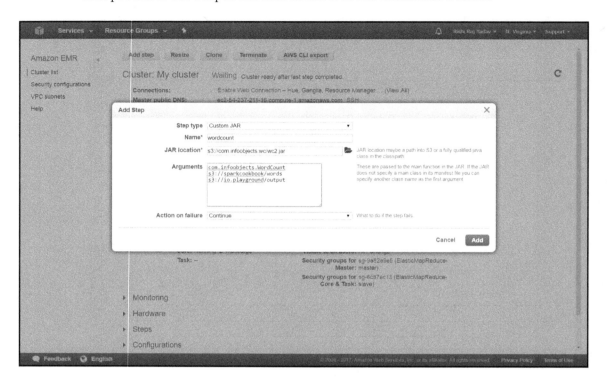

7. The **wordcount** step's status will change to completed, indicating a successful completion of the step, as shown in the following screenshot:

8. The output will be created and stored in the given S3 location. Here, it is in the output folder under the `io.playground` bucket:

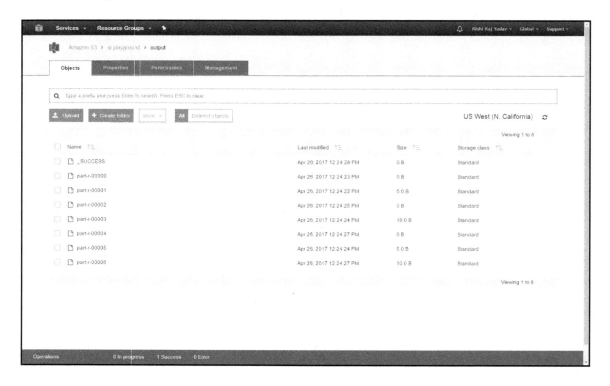

How it works...

Let's look at the options shown in step 3:

- **Cluster name**: This is where you provide an appropriate name for the cluster.
- **S3 folder**: This is the folder location where the S3 bucket's logs for this cluster will go to.
- **Launch mode**:
    - **Cluster**: The cluster will continue to run until you terminate it.
    - **Step execution**: This is to add steps after the application is launched.

- **Software configuration**:
    - **Vendor**: This is Amazon EMI with the open source Hadoop versus MapR's version.
    - **Release**: This is self-evident.
    - **Applications**:
        - **Core Hadoop**: This is focused on the SQL interface.
        - **HBase**: This is focused on partial no-SQL-oriented workloads.
        - **Presto**: This is focused on ad-hoc query processing.
        - **Spark**: This is focused on Spark.

- **Hardware configuration**:
    - **Instance type**: This topic will be covered in detail in the next section.
    - **Number of instances**: This refers to the number of nodes in the cluster. One of them will be the master node and the rest slave nodes.

- **Security and access**:
    - **EC2 key pair**: You can associate an EC2 key pair with the cluster that you can use to connect to it via SSH.
    - **Permissions**: You can allow other users besides the default Hadoop user to submit jobs.
    - **EMR role**: This allows EMR to call other AWS services, such as EC2, on your behalf.
    - **EC2 instance profile**: This provides access to other AWS services, such as S3 and DynamoDB, via the EC2 instances that are launched by EMR.

EC2 instance types

EC2 instances are the most expensive part of a company's AWS bill. So, selecting the right instance type is the key through which you can optimize your bill. The following section is a quick overview of the different instance types. Instance types, both in the cloud and on premises, are defined by four factors:

- Number of cores
- Memory
- Storage (size and type)
- Network performance

To see a quick illustration of how these factors affect each other, visit `http://youtube.com/infoobjects`.

In the EC2 world, these factors have been modified slightly to vCPU. vCPU is a virtualized unit of:

- Memory
- Storage (size and type)
- Network performance

Instance type families are defined by the ratio of these factors, especially vCPU to memory. In a given family, this ratio remains unchanged (T2 excluded). Different instance families serve different purposes, almost like different types of automobiles. In fact, we are going to use the automobile metaphor in this section to illustrate these families.

T2 - Free Tier Burstable (EBS only)

The T2 instance type is a gateway drug in the AWS world, the reason being it belongs to Free Tier. Developers who sign up for AWS get this instance type for up to a year. This tier has six subtypes:

Instance Type	vCPUs	CPU Credit/Hr	Memory (GiB)
t2.micro	1	6	1
t2.small	1	12	2
t2.medium	2	24	4
t2.large	2	36	6
t2.xlarge	4	54	6
t2.2xlarge	8	81	32

M4 - General purpose (EBS only)

M4 is the instance type you use when in doubt. Developers who sign up for AWS get this instance type for up to a year. This tier has six subtypes:

Instance Type	vCPUs	Memory (GiB)	Dedicated Bandwidth
m4.large	2	8	450 mbps
m4.xlarge	4	16	750 mbps

m4.2xlarge	8	32	1,000 mbps
m4.4xlarge	16	64	2,000 mbps
m4.10xlarge	40	160	4,000 mbps
m4.16xlarge	64	256	10,000 mbps

C4 - Compute optimized

This tier has five subtypes:

Instance Type	vCPUs	Memory (GiB)	Dedicated Bandwidth
c4.large	2	3.75	500 mbps
c4.xlarge	4	7.5	750 mbps
c4.2xlarge	8	15	1,000 mbps
c4.4xlarge	16	30	2,000 mbps
c4.8xlarge	36	60	4,000 mbps

X1 - Memory optimized

This tier has two subtypes:

Instance Type	vCPUs	Memory (GiB)	Dedicated Bandwidth
x1.16xlarge	2	8	450 mbps
x1.32xlarge	4	16	750 mbps

R4 - Memory optimized

This tier has six subtypes:

Instance Type	vCPUs	Memory (GiB)	Dedicated Bandwidth
r4.large	2	15.25	10 gbps
r4.xlarge	4	30.5	10 gbps
r4.2xlarge	8	61	10 gbps
r4.4xlarge	16	122	10 gbps
r4.8xlarge	32	244	10 gbps
r4.16xlarge	64	488	20 gbps

P2 - General purpose GPU

This tier has three subtypes:

Instance Type	vCPUs	Memory (GiB)	GPUs	GPU Memory (GiB)
p2.xlarge	4	61	1	12
p2.8xlarge	32	488	8	96
p2.16xlarge	64	732	16	192

I3 - Storage optimized

This tier has six subtypes:

Instance Type	vCPUs	Memory (GiB)	Storage (GB)
i3.large	2	15.25	475 NVMe SSD
i3.xlarge	4	30.5	950 NVMe SSD
i3.2xlarge	8	61	1,900 NVMe SSD
i3.4xlarge	16	122	2x1,900 NVMe SSD
i3.8xlarge	32	244	4x1,900 NVMe SSD
i3.16xlarge	64	488	8x1,900 NVMe SSD

D2 - Storage optimized

This tier is for **massively parallel processing** (**MPP**), data warehouse, and so on type usage. This tier has four subtypes:

Instance Type	vCPUs	Memory (GiB)	Storage (GB)
d2.xlarge	4	30.5	3x2000 HDD
d2.2xlarge	8	61	6x2000 HDD
d2.4xlarge	16	122	12x2000 HDD
d2.8xlarge	32	244	24x2000 HDD

Installing Spark from binaries

You can build Spark from the source code, or you can download precompiled binaries from http://spark.apache.org. For a standard use case, binaries are good enough, and this recipe will focus on installing Spark using binaries.

Getting ready

At the time of writing, Spark's current version is 2.1. Please check the latest version from Spark's download page at http://spark.apache.org/downloads.html. Binaries are developed with the most recent and stable version of Hadoop. To use a specific version of Hadoop, the recommended approach is that you build it from sources, which we will cover in the next recipe.

All the recipes in this book are developed using Ubuntu Linux, but they should work fine on any POSIX environment. Spark expects Java to be installed and the JAVA_HOME environment variable set.

In Linux/Unix systems, there are certain standards for the location of files and directories, which we are going to follow in this book. The following is a quick cheat sheet:

Directory	Description
/bin	This stores essential command binaries
/etc	This is where host-specific system configurations are located
/opt	This is where add-on application software packages are located
/var	This is where variable data is located
/tmp	This stores the temporary files
/home	This is where user home directories are located

How to do it...

Here are the installation steps:

1. Open the terminal and download the binaries using the following command:

```
$ wget
http://d3kbcqa49mib13.cloudfront.net/spark-2.1.0-bin-hadoop2.7.tgz
```

2. Unpack the binaries:

```
$ tar -zxf spark-2.1.0-bin-hadoop2.7.tgz
```

3. Rename the folder containing the binaries by stripping the version information:

```
$ sudo mv spark-2.1.0-bin-hadoop2.7 spark
```

4. Move the configuration folder to the /etc folder so that it can be turned into a symbolic link later:

```
$ sudo mv spark/conf/* /etc/spark
```

5. Create your company-specific installation directory under /opt. As the recipes in this book are tested on the infoobjects sandbox, use infoobjects as the directory name. Create the /opt/infoobjects directory:

```
$ sudo mkdir -p /opt/infoobjects
```

6. Move the spark directory to /opt/infoobjects, as it's an add-on software package:

```
$ sudo mv spark /opt/infoobjects/
```

7. Change the permissions of the spark home directory, namely 0755 = user:read-write-execute group:read-execute world:read-execute:

```
$ sudo chmod -R 755 /opt/infoobjects/spark
```

8. Move to the spark home directory:

```
$ cd /opt/infoobjects/spark
```

9. Create the symbolic link:

```
$ sudo ln -s /etc/spark conf
```

10. Append Spark binaries path to PATH in .bashrc:

```
$ echo "export PATH=$PATH:/opt/infoobjects/spark/bin" >>
/home/hduser/.bashrc
```

11. Open a new terminal.

12. Create the log directory in /var:

```
$ sudo mkdir -p /var/log/spark
```

13. Make hduser the owner of Spark's log directory:

```
$ sudo chown -R hduser:hduser /var/log/spark
```

14. Create Spark's `tmp` directory:

```
$ mkdir /tmp/spark
```

15. Configure Spark with the help of the following command lines:

```
$ cd /etc/spark
$ echo "export HADOOP_CONF_DIR=/opt/infoobjects/hadoop/etc/hadoop" >>
spark-env.sh
$ echo "export YARN_CONF_DIR=/opt/infoobjects/hadoop/etc/Hadoop" >>
spark-env.sh
$ echo "export SPARK_LOG_DIR=/var/log/spark" >> spark-env.sh
$ echo "export SPARK_WORKER_DIR=/tmp/spark" >> spark-env.sh
```

16. Change the ownership of the `spark` home directory to `root`:

```
$ sudo chown -R root:root /opt/infoobjects/spark
```

Building the Spark source code with Maven

Installing Spark using binaries works fine in most cases. For advanced cases, such as the following (but not limited to), compiling from the source code is a better option:

- Compiling for a specific Hadoop version
- Adding the Hive integration
- Adding the YARN integration

Getting ready

The following are the prerequisites for this recipe to work:

- Java 1.8 or a later version
- Maven 3.x

How to do it...

The following are the steps to build the Spark source code with Maven:

1. Increase `MaxPermSize` of the heap:

    ```
    $ echo "export _JAVA_OPTIONS="-XX:MaxPermSize=1G""  >>
    /home/hduser/.bashrc
    ```

2. Open a new terminal window and download the Spark source code from GitHub:

    ```
    $ wget https://github.com/apache/spark/archive/branch-2.1.zip
    ```

3. Unpack the archive:

    ```
    $ unzip branch-2.1.zip
    ```

4. Rename unzipped folder to `spark`:

    ```
    $ mv spark-branch-2.1 spark
    ```

5. Move to the `spark` directory:

    ```
    $ cd spark
    ```

6. Compile the sources with the YARN-enabled, Hadoop version 2.7, and Hive-enabled flags and skip the tests for faster compilation:

    ```
    $ mvn -Pyarn -Phadoop-2.7 -Dhadoop.version=2.7.0 -Phive -
    DskipTests clean package
    ```

7. Move the `conf` folder to the `etc` folder so that it can be turned into a symbolic link:

    ```
    $ sudo mv spark/conf /etc/
    ```

8. Move the `spark` directory to `/opt` as it's an add-on software package:

    ```
    $ sudo mv spark /opt/infoobjects/spark
    ```

9. Change the ownership of the `spark` home directory to `root`:

    ```
    $ sudo chown -R root:root /opt/infoobjects/spark
    ```

10. Change the permissions of the `spark` home directory, namely `0755 = user:rwx group:r-x world:r-x`:

    ```
    $ sudo chmod -R 755 /opt/infoobjects/spark
    ```

11. Move to the `spark` home directory:

    ```
    $ cd /opt/infoobjects/spark
    ```

12. Create a symbolic link:

    ```
    $ sudo ln -s /etc/spark conf
    ```

13. Put the Spark executable in the path by editing `.bashrc`:

    ```
    $ echo "export PATH=$PATH:/opt/infoobjects/spark/bin" >>
      /home/hduser/.bashrc
    ```

14. Create the `log` directory in `/var`:

    ```
    $ sudo mkdir -p /var/log/spark
    ```

15. Make `hduser` the owner of Spark's `log` directory:

    ```
    $ sudo chown -R hduser:hduser /var/log/spark
    ```

16. Create Spark's `tmp` directory:

    ```
    $ mkdir /tmp/spark
    ```

17. Configure Spark with the help of the following command lines:

    ```
    $ cd /etc/spark
    $ echo "export HADOOP_CONF_DIR=/opt/infoobjects/hadoop/etc/hadoop"
        >> spark-env.sh
    $ echo "export YARN_CONF_DIR=/opt/infoobjects/hadoop/etc/Hadoop"
        >> spark-env.sh
    $ echo "export SPARK_LOG_DIR=/var/log/spark" >> spark-env.sh
    $ echo "export SPARK_WORKER_DIR=/tmp/spark" >> spark-env.sh
    ```

Launching Spark on Amazon EC2

Amazon Elastic Compute Cloud (**Amazon EC2**) is a web service that provides resizable compute instances in the cloud. Amazon EC2 provides the following features:

- On-demand delivery of IT resources via the Internet
- Provisioning of as many instances as you like
- Payment for the hours during which you use instances, such as your utility bill
- No setup cost, no installation, and no overhead at all
- Shutting down or terminating instances when you no longer need them
- Making such instances available on familiar operating systems

EC2 provides different types of instances to meet all your compute needs, such as general-purpose instances, microinstances, memory-optimized instances, storage-optimized instances, and others. They also have a Free Tier of microinstances for trial purposes.

Getting ready

The `spark-ec2` script comes bundled with Spark and makes it easy to launch, manage, and shut down clusters on Amazon EC2.

Before you start, do the following things: log in to the Amazon AWS account via `http://aws.amazon.com`.

1. Click on **Security Credentials** under your account name in the top-right corner.
2. Click on **Access Keys** and **Create New Access Key**:

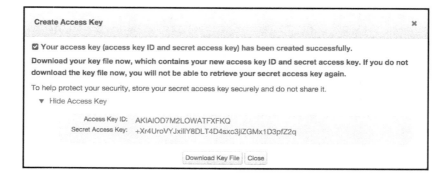

3. Download the key file (let's save it in the `/home/hduser/kp` folder as `spark-kp1.pem`).

4. Set permissions on the key file to `600`.

5. Set environment variables to reflect **access key ID** and **secret access key** (replace the sample values with your own values):

```
$ echo "export AWS_ACCESS_KEY_ID="AKIAOD7M2LOWATFXFKQ"" >>
/home/hduser/.bashrc
$ echo "export
AWS_SECRET_ACCESS_KEY="+Xr4UroVYJxiLiY8DLT4DLT4D4sxc3ijZGMx1D3pfZ2q"" >>
        /home/hduser/.bashrc
$ echo "export PATH=$PATH:/opt/infoobjects/spark/ec2" >>
/home/hduser/.bashrc
```

How to do it...

1. Spark comes bundled with scripts to launch the Spark cluster on Amazon EC2. Let's launch the cluster using the following command:

```
        $ cd /home/hduser
$ spark-ec2 -k <key-pair> -i <key-file> -s <num-slaves> launch <cluster-name>
<key-pair> - name of EC2 keypair created in AWS
<key-file> the private key file you downloaded
<num-slaves> number of slave nodes to launch
<cluster-name> name of the cluster
```

2. Launch the cluster with the example value:

```
        $ spark-ec2 -k kp-spark -i /home/hduser/keypairs/kp-spark.pem --hadoop-major-
        version 2  -s 3 launch spark-cluster
```

3. Sometimes, the default availability zones are not available; in that case, retry sending the request by specifying the specific availability zone you are requesting:

```
        $ spark-ec2 -k kp-spark -i /home/hduser/keypairs/kp-spark.pem -z
us-east-1b --
        hadoop-major-version 2  -s 3 launch spark-cluster
```

4. If your application needs to retain data after the instance shuts down, attach EBS volume to it (for example, 10 GB space):

```
$ spark-ec2 -k kp-spark -i /home/hduser/keypairs/kp-spark.pem --
hadoop-major-
        version 2 -ebs-vol-size 10 -s 3 launch spark-cluster
```

5. If you use Amazon's spot instances, here is the way to do it:

```
$ spark-ec2 -k kp-spark -i /home/hduser/keypairs/kp-spark.pem -
spot-price=0.15
        --hadoop-major-version 2  -s 3 launch spark-cluster
```

 Spot instances allow you to name your own price for Amazon EC2's computing capacity. You simply bid for spare Amazon EC2 instances and run them whenever your bid exceeds the current spot price, which varies in real time and is based on supply and demand (source: www.amazon.com).

6. After completing the preceding launch process, check the status of the cluster by going to the **webUI** URL that will be printed at the end:

```
Connection to ec2-54-211-128-216.compute-1.amazonaws.com closed.
Spark standalone cluster started at http://ec2-54-211-128-216.compute-1.amazonaws.com:8080
Ganglia started at http://ec2-54-211-128-216.compute-1.amazonaws.com:5080/ganglia
Done!
```

7. Check the status of the cluster:

Spark **Spark Master at spark://ec2-54-211-128-216.compute-1.amazonaws.com:7077**

URL: spark://ec2-54-211-128-216.compute-1.amazonaws.com:7077
Workers: 3
Cores: 6 Total, 0 Used
Memory: 18.8 GB Total, 0.0 B Used
Applications: 0 Running, 0 Completed
Drivers: 0 Running, 0 Completed
Status: ALIVE

Workers

Id	Address	State	Cores	Memory
worker-20141130022618-ip-10-170-8-91.ec2.internal-59489	ip-10-170-8-91.ec2.internal:59489	ALIVE	2 (0 Used)	6.3 GB (0.0 B Used)
worker-20141130022618-ip-10-182-148-55.ec2.internal-51719	ip-10-182-148-55.ec2.internal:51719	ALIVE	2 (0 Used)	6.3 GB (0.0 B Used)
worker-20141130022618-ip-10-182-183-44.ec2.internal-46837	ip-10-182-183-44.ec2.internal:46837	ALIVE	2 (0 Used)	6.3 GB (0.0 B Used)

Running Applications

ID	Name	Cores	Memory per Node	Submitted Time	User	State	Duration

Completed Applications

ID	Name	Cores	Memory per Node	Submitted Time	User	State	Duration

8. Now, to access the Spark cluster on EC2, connect to the master node using **secure shell protocol (SSH)**:

```
$ spark-ec2 -k spark-kp1 -i /home/hduser/kp/spark-kp1.pem  login
spark-cluster
```

9. The following image illustrates the result you'll get:

```
hduser@infoobjects:~$ spark-ec2 -k spark-kp1 -i /home/hduser/kp/spark-kp1.pem  login spark-cluster
Searching for existing cluster spark-cluster...
Found 1 master(s), 3 slaves
Logging into master ec2-54-211-128-216.compute-1.amazonaws.com...
Last login: Sun Nov 30 02:22:36 2014 from c-73-162-232-122.hsd1.ca.comcast.net

    __|  __|_  )
    _|  (     /   Amazon Linux AMI
   ___|\___|___|

https://aws.amazon.com/amazon-linux-ami/2013.03-release-notes/
There are 75 security update(s) out of 282 total update(s) available
Run "sudo yum update" to apply all updates.
Amazon Linux version 2014.09 is available.
root@ip-10-182-135-159 ~]$ ls
ephemeral-hdfs  hadoop-native  mapreduce  persistent-hdfs  scala  shark  spark  spark-ec2  tachyon
```

10. Check the directories in the master node and see what they do:

Directory	Description
ephemeral-hdfs	This is the Hadoop instance for which data is ephemeral and gets deleted when you stop or restart the machine.
persistent-hdfs	Each node has a very small amount of persistent storage (approximately 3 GB). If you use this instance, data will be retained in that space.
hadoop-native	This refers to the native libraries that support Hadoop, such as snappy compression libraries.
scala	This refers to the Scala installation.
shark	This refers to the Shark installation (Shark is no longer supported and is replaced by Spark SQL).
spark	This refers to the Spark installation.
spark-ec2	This refers to the files that support this cluster deployment.
tachyon	This refers to the Tachyon installation.

11. Check the HDFS version in an ephemeral instance:

```
$ ephemeral-hdfs/bin/hadoop version
Hadoop 2.0.0-chd4.2.0
```

12. Check the HDFS version in a persistent instance with the following command:

```
$ persistent-hdfs/bin/hadoop version
Hadoop 2.0.0-chd4.2.0
```

13. Change the configuration level of the logs:

```
$ cd spark/conf
```

14. The default log level information is too verbose, so let's change it to Error:

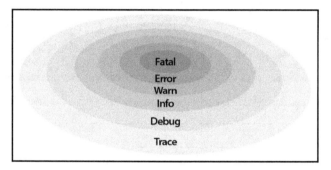

- Create the `log4.properties` file by renaming the template:

```
$ mv log4j.properties.template log4j.properties
```

- Open `log4j.properties` in vi or your favorite editor:

```
$ vi log4j.properties
```

- Change the second line from | `log4j.rootCategory=INFO, console` to | `log4j.rootCategory=ERROR, console`.

15. Copy the configuration to all the slave nodes after the change:

```
$ spark-ec2/copydir spark/conf
```

16. You should get something like this:

```
root@ip-10-168-32-181 ~]$ spark-ec2/copy-dir spark/conf/
RSYNC'ing /root/spark/conf to slaves...
ec2-174-129-51-11.compute-1.amazonaws.com
ec2-107-20-52-62.compute-1.amazonaws.com
ec2-54-224-17-251.compute-1.amazonaws.com
```

17. Destroy the Spark cluster:

```
$ spark-ec2 destroy spark-cluster
```

See also

- http://aws.amazon.com/ec2

Deploying Spark on a cluster in standalone mode

Compute resources in a distributed environment need to be managed so that resource utilization is efficient and every job gets a fair chance to run. Spark comes with its own cluster manager, which is conveniently called standalone mode. Spark also supports working with YARN and Mesos cluster managers.

The cluster manager you choose should be mostly driven by both legacy concerns and whether other frameworks, such as MapReduce, share the same compute resource pool. If your cluster has legacy MapReduce jobs running and all of them cannot be converted into Spark jobs, it is a good idea to use YARN as the cluster manager. Mesos is emerging as a data center operating system to conveniently manage jobs across frameworks, and it is very compatible with Spark.

If the Spark framework is the only framework in your cluster, then the standalone mode is good enough. As Spark is evolving as a technology, you will see more and more use cases of Spark being used as the standalone framework, serving all your big data compute needs. For example, some jobs may use Apache Mahout at present because `MLlib` does not have a specific machine-learning library, which the job needs. As soon as `MLlib` gets its library, this particular job can be moved to Spark.

Getting ready

Let's consider a cluster of six nodes as an example setup--one master and five slaves (replace them with the actual node names in your cluster):

```
     Master
m1.zettabytes.com
Slaves
s1.zettabytes.com
s2.zettabytes.com
s3.zettabytes.com
s4.zettabytes.com
s5.zettabytes.com
```

How to do it...

1. Since Spark's standalone mode is the default, all you need to do is have Spark binaries installed on both master and slave machines. Put `/opt/infoobjects/spark/sbin` in the path on every node:

```
$ echo "export PATH=$PATH:/opt/infoobjects/spark/sbin" >>
/home/hduser/.bashrc
```

2. Start the standalone master server (SSH to master first):

```
hduser@m1.zettabytes.com~] start-master.sh
```

Master, by default, starts on port 7077, which slaves use to connect to it. It also has a web UI at port 8088.

3. Connect to the master node using a **Secure Shell (SSH)** connection and then start the slaves:

```
hduser@s1.zettabytes.com~] spark-class
org.apache.spark.deploy.worker.Worker
          spark://m1.zettabytes.com:7077
```

Argument	Meaning
`-h <ipaddress/HOST>` and `--host <ipaddress/HOST>`	IP address/DNS service to listen on
`-p <port>` and `--port <port>`	Port for the service to listen on
`--webui-port <port>`	This is the port for the web UI (by default, 8080 is for the master and 8081 for the worker)
`-c <cores>` and `--cores <cores>`	These refer to the total CPU core Spark applications that can be used on a machine (worker only)
`-m <memory>` and `--memory <memory>`	These refer to the total RAM Spark applications that can be used on a machine (worker only)
`-d <dir>` and `--work-dir <dir>`	These refer to the directory to use for scratch space and job output logs

For fine-grained configuration, the above parameters work with both master and slaves. Rather than manually starting master and slave daemons on each node, it can also be accomplished using cluster launch scripts. Cluster launch scripts are outside the scope of this book. Please refer to books about Chef or Puppet.

4. First, create the `conf/slaves` file on a master node and add one line per slave hostname (using an example of five slave nodes, replace the following slave DNS with the DNS of the slave nodes in your cluster):

```
hduser@m1.zettabytes.com~] echo "s1.zettabytes.com" >> conf/slaves
hduser@m1.zettabytes.com~] echo "s2.zettabytes.com" >> conf/slaves
hduser@m1.zettabytes.com~] echo "s3.zettabytes.com" >> conf/slaves
hduser@m1.zettabytes.com~] echo "s4.zettabytes.com" >> conf/slaves
hduser@m1.zettabytes.com~] echo "s5.zettabytes.com" >> conf/slaves
```

Once the slave machine is set up, you can call the following scripts to start/stop the cluster:

Script name	Purpose
`start-master.sh`	Starts a master instance on the host machine
`start-slaves.sh`	Starts a slave instance on each node of the slaves file
`start-all.sh`	Starts both the master and slaves
`stop-master.sh`	Stops the master instance on the host machine
`stop-slaves.sh`	Stops the slave instance on all the nodes of the slaves file
`stop-all.sh`	Stops both the master and slaves

5. Connect an application to the cluster through `Scala code`:

```
val sparkContext = new SparkContext(new
    SparkConf().setMaster("spark://m1.zettabytes.com:7077")Setting
master URL for
        spark-shell
```

6. Connect to the cluster through `Spark shell`:

```
$ spark-shell --master spark://master:7077
```

How it works...

In standalone mode, Spark follows the master-slave architecture, very much like Hadoop, MapReduce, and YARN. The compute master daemon is called **Spark master** and runs on one master node. Spark master can be made highly available using ZooKeeper. You can also add more standby masters on the fly if needed.

The compute slave daemon is called a **worker**, and it exists on each slave node. The worker daemon does the following:

- Reports the availability of the compute resources on a slave node, such as the number of cores, memory, and others, to the Spark master
- Spawns the executor when asked to do so by the Spark master
- Restarts the executor if it dies

There is, at most, one executor per application, per slave machine.

Both Spark master and the worker are very lightweight. Typically, memory allocation between 500 MB to 1 GB is sufficient. This value can be set in `conf/spark-env.sh` by setting the `SPARK_DAEMON_MEMORY` parameter. For example, the following configuration will set the memory to 1 gigabits for both the master and worker daemon. Make sure you have `sudo` as the super user before running it:

```
$ echo "export SPARK_DAEMON_MEMORY=1g" >>
/opt/infoobjects/spark/conf/spark-env.sh
```

By default, each slave node has one worker instance running on it. Sometimes, you may have a few machines that are more powerful than others. In that case, you can spawn more than one worker on that machine with the following configuration (only on those machines):

```
$ echo "export SPARK_WORKER_INSTANCES=2" >>
/opt/infoobjects/spark/conf/spark-env.sh
```

The Spark worker, by default, uses all the cores on the slave machine for its executors. If you would like to limit the number of cores the worker could use, you can set it to the number of your choice (for example, 12), using the following configuration:

```
$ echo "export SPARK_WORKER_CORES=12" >>
/opt/infoobjects/spark/conf/spark-env.sh
```

The Spark worker, by default, uses all of the available RAM (1 GB for executors). Note that you cannot allocate how much memory each specific executor will use (you can control this from the driver configuration). To assign another value to the total memory (for example, 24 GB) to be used by all the executors combined, execute the following setting:

```
$ echo "export SPARK_WORKER_MEMORY=24g" >>
/opt/infoobjects/spark/conf/spark-env.sh
```

There are some settings you can do at the driver level:

- To specify the maximum number of CPU cores to be used by a given application across the cluster, you can set the `spark.cores.max` configuration in `Spark submit` or `Spark shell` as follows:

```
$ spark-submit --conf spark.cores.max=12
```

- To specify the amount of memory that each executor should be allocated (the minimum recommendation is 8 GB), you can set the `spark.executor.memory` configuration in `Spark submit` or `Spark shell` as follows:

```
$ spark-submit --conf spark.executor.memory=8g
```

The following diagram depicts the high-level architecture of a Spark cluster:

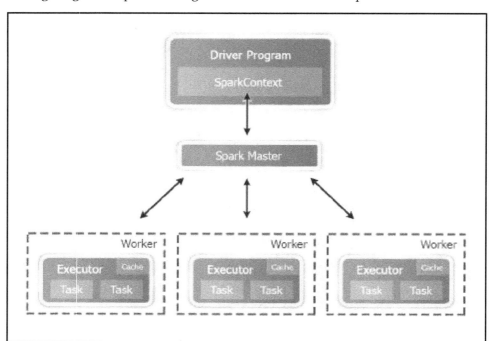

See also

To find more configuration options, refer to the following URL:

- http://spark.apache.org/docs/latest/spark-standalone.html

Deploying Spark on a cluster with Mesos

Mesos is slowly emerging as a data center operating system for managing all the compute resources across a data center. Mesos runs on any computer running the Linux operating system. It is built using the same principles as the Linux kernel. Let's see how we can install Mesos.

How to do it...

Mesosphere provides a binary distribution of Mesos. The most recent package of the `Mesos` distribution can be installed from the Mesosphere repositories by performing the following steps:

1. Execute Mesos on a Ubuntu OS with the trusty version:

```
$ sudo apt-key adv --keyserver keyserver.ubuntu.com --recv E56151BF
    DISTRO=$(lsb_release -is | tr '[:upper:]' '[:lower:]')
CODENAME=$(lsb_release
        -cs)
$ sudo vi /etc/apt/sources.list.d/mesosphere.list
deb http://repos.mesosphere.io/Ubuntu trusty main
```

2. Update the repositories:

```
$ sudo apt-get -y update
```

3. Install Mesos:

```
$ sudo apt-get -y install mesos
```

4. To connect Spark to Mesos and to integrate Spark with Mesos, make Spark binaries available to Mesos and configure the Spark driver to connect to Mesos.

5. Use the Spark binaries from the first recipe and upload them to HDFS:

```
$ hdfs dfs -put spark-2.1.0-bin-hadoop2.7.tgz spark-2.1.0-bin-
hadoop2.7.tgz
```

6. The master URL of a single master Mesos is `mesos://host:5050`; the master URL of a ZooKeeper-managed Mesos cluster is `mesos://zk://host:2181`.

7. Set the following variables in `spark-env.sh`:

```
$ sudo vi spark-env.sh
export MESOS_NATIVE_LIBRARY=/usr/local/lib/libmesos.so
export SPARK_EXECUTOR_URI= hdfs://localhost:9000/user/hduser/spark-2.1.0-
bin-
        hadoop2.7.tgz
```

8. Run the following commands from the Scala program:

```
Val conf = new SparkConf().setMaster("mesos://host:5050")
Val sparkContext = new SparkContext(conf)
```

9. Run the following command from the Spark shell:

```
$ spark-shell --master mesos://host:5050
```

Mesos has two run modes:

- **Fine-grained**: In the fine-grained (default) mode, every Spark task runs as a separate Mesos task.

- **Coarse-grained**: This mode will launch only one long-running Spark task on each Mesos machine

10. To run in the coarse-grained mode, set the spark.mesos.coarse property:

```
Conf.set("spark.mesos.coarse","true")
```

Deploying Spark on a cluster with YARN

Yet Another Resource Negotiator (**YARN**) is Hadoop's compute framework that runs on top of HDFS, which is Hadoop's storage layer.

YARN follows the master-slave architecture. The master daemon is called ResourceManager and the slave daemon is called NodeManager. Besides this application, life cycle management is done by ApplicationMaster, which can be spawned on any slave node and would be alive during the lifetime of an application.

When Spark is run on YARN, ResourceManager performs the role of the Spark master and NodeManagers works as executor nodes.

While running Spark with YARN, each Spark executor is run as a YARN container.

Getting ready

Running Spark on YARN requires a binary distribution of Spark that has YARN support. In both the Spark installation recipes, we have taken care of this.

How to do it...

1. To run Spark on YARN, the first step is to set the configuration:

```
        HADOOP_CONF_DIR: to write to HDFS
YARN_CONF_DIR: to connect to YARN ResourceManager
$ cd /opt/infoobjects/spark/conf (or /etc/spark)
$ sudo vi spark-env.sh
export HADOOP_CONF_DIR=/opt/infoobjects/hadoop/etc/Hadoop
export YARN_CONF_DIR=/opt/infoobjects/hadoop/etc/hadoop
```

- You can see this in the following screenshot:

```
#!/usr/bin/env bash

# This file contains environment variables required to run Spark. Copy it as
# spark-env.sh and edit that to configure Spark for your site.
#
# The following variables can be set in this file:
# - SPARK_LOCAL_IP, to set the IP address Spark binds to on this node
# - MESOS_NATIVE_LIBRARY, to point to your libmesos.so if you use Mesos
# - SPARK_JAVA_OPTS, to set node-specific JVM options for Spark. Note that
#   we recommend setting app-wide options in the application's driver program.
#     Examples of node-specific options : -Dspark.local.dir, GC options
#     Examples of app-wide options : -Dspark.serializer
#
# If using the standalone deploy mode, you can also set variables for it here:
# - SPARK_MASTER_IP, to bind the master to a different IP address or hostname
# - SPARK_MASTER_PORT / SPARK_MASTER_WEBUI_PORT, to use non-default ports
# - SPARK_WORKER_CORES, to set the number of cores to use on this machine
# - SPARK_WORKER_MEMORY, to set how much memory to use (e.g. 1000m, 2g)
# - SPARK_WORKER_PORT / SPARK_WORKER_WEBUI_PORT
# - SPARK_WORKER_INSTANCES, to set the number of worker processes per node
# - SPARK_WORKER_DIR, to set the working directory of worker processes
export HADOOP_CONF_DIR=/opt/infoobjects/hadoop/etc/hadoop
export YARN_CONF_DIR=/opt/infoobjects/hadoop/etc/hadoop
export SPARK_LOG_DIR=/var/log/spark
export SPARK_WORKER_DIR=/var/spark/worker
```

2. The following command launches YARN Spark in the yarn-client mode:

```
$ spark-submit --class path.to.your.Class --master yarn --deploy-mode client
    [options] <app jar> [app options]
```

Here's an example:

```
$ spark-submit --class com.infoobjects.TwitterFireHose --master
yarn --deploy-
    mode client --num-executors 3 --driver-memory 4g --executor-
memory 2g --
        executor-cores 1 target/sparkio.jar 10
```

3. The following command launches `Spark shell` in the `yarn-client` mode:

```
$ spark-shell --master yarn --deploy-mode client
```

4. The command to launch the spark application in the `yarn-cluster` mode is as follows:

```
$ spark-submit --class path.to.your.Class --master yarn --deploy-
mode cluster
    [options] <app jar> [app options]
```

Here's an example:

```
$ spark-submit --class com.infoobjects.TwitterFireHose --master
yarn --deploy-
    mode cluster --num-executors 3 --driver-memory 4g --executor-
memory 2g --
        executor-cores 1 target/sparkio.jar 10
```

How it works...

Spark applications on YARN run in two modes:

- `yarn-client`: Spark Driver runs in the client process outside of the YARN cluster, and `ApplicationMaster` is only used to negotiate the resources from `ResourceManager`.
- `yarn-cluster`: Spark Driver runs in `ApplicationMaster`, spawned by `NodeManager` on a slave node.

The `yarn-cluster` mode is recommended for production deployments, while the `yarn-client` mode is good for development and debugging, where you would like to see the immediate output. There is no need to specify the Spark master in either mode as it's picked from the Hadoop configuration, and the master parameter is either `yarn-client` or `yarn-cluster`.

The following figure shows how Spark is run with YARN in the client mode:

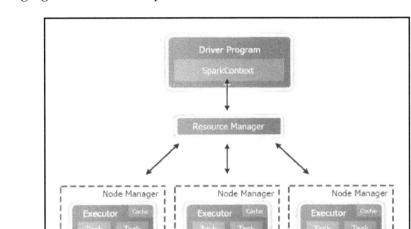

The following figure shows how Spark is run with YARN in the cluster mode:

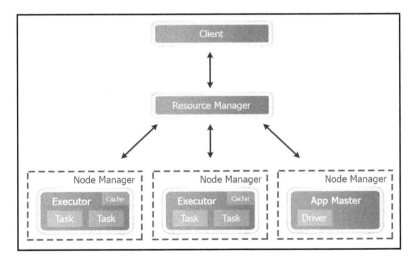

In the YARN mode, the following configuration parameters can be set:

- `--num-executors`: To configure how many executors will be allocated
- `--executor-memory`: RAM per executor
- `--executor-cores`: CPU cores per executor

Understanding SparkContext and SparkSession

SparkContext and SparkSession are the entry points into the world of Spark, so it is important you understand both well.

SparkContext

SparkContext is the first object that a Spark program must create to access the cluster. In `spark-shell`, it is directly accessible via `spark.sparkContext`. Here's how you can programmatically create SparkContext in your Scala code:

```
import org.apache.spark.SparkContext
import org.apache.spark.SparkConf
val conf = new SparkConf().setAppName("my app").setMaster("master url")
new SparkContext(conf)
```

SparkSession

SparkContext, though still supported, was more relevant in the case of RDD (covered in the next recipe). As you will see in the rest of the book, different libraries have different wrappers around SparkContext, for example, HiveContext/SQLContext for Spark SQL, StreamingContext for Streaming, and so on. As all the libraries are moving toward DataSet/DataFrame, it makes sense to have a unified entry point for all these libraries as well, and that is `SparkSession`. SparkSession is available as `spark` in the `spark-shell`. Here's how you do it:

```
import org.apache.spark.SparkContext
import org.apache.spark.SparkConf
val sparkSession = SparkSession.builder.master("master url").appName("my app").getOrCreate()
```

Understanding resilient distributed dataset - RDD

Though RDD is getting replaced with DataFrame/DataSet-based APIs, there are still a lot of APIs that have not been migrated yet. In this recipe, we will look at how the concept of lineage works in RDD.

Externally, RDD is a distributed, immutable collection of objects. Internally, it consists of the following five parts:

- Set of partitions (`rdd.getPartitions`)
- List of dependencies on parent RDDs (`rdd.dependencies`)
- Function to compute a partition, given its parents
- Partitioner, which is optional (`rdd.partitioner`)
- Preferred location of each partition, which is optional (`rdd.preferredLocations`)

The first three are needed for an RDD to be recomputed in case data is lost. When combined, it is called **lineage**. The last two parts are optimizations.

A set of partitions is how data is divided into nodes. In the case of HDFS, it means `InputSplits`, which are mostly the same as the block (except when a record crosses block boundaries; in that case, it will be slightly bigger than a block).

How to do it...

Let's revisit our word count example to understand these five parts. This is how an RDD graph looks for **wordCount** at the dataset level view:

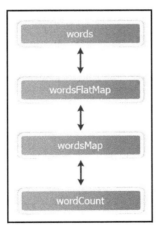

Basically, this is how the flow goes:

1. Load the `words` folder as an RDD:

```
scala> val words =
sc.textFile("hdfs://localhost:9000/user/hduser/words")
```

The following are the five parts of the `words` RDD:

Part	Description
Partitions	One partition per HDFS inputsplit/block (`org.apache.spark.rdd.HadoopPartition`)
Dependencies	None
Compute function	To read the block
Preferred location	The HDFS block's location
Partitioner	None

2. Tokenize the words of the `words` RDD with each word on a separate line:

```
scala> val wordsFlatMap = words.flatMap(_.split("W+"))
```

The following are the five parts of the `wordsFlatMap` RDD:

Part	Description
Partitions	Same as the parent RDD, that is, `words` (`org.apache.spark.rdd.HadoopPartition`)
Dependencies	Same as the parent RDD, that is, `words` (`org.apache.spark.OneToOneDependency`)
Compute function	To compute the parent and split each element, which flattens the results
Preferred location	Ask parent RDD
Partitioner	None

3. Transform each word in the `wordsFlatMap` RDD into the (word,1) tuple:

```
scala> val wordsMap = wordsFlatMap.map( w => (w,1))
```

The following are the five parts of the `wordsMap` RDD:

Part	Description
Partitions	Same as the parent RDD, that is, wordsFlatMap (org.apache.spark.rdd.HadoopPartition)
Dependencies	Same as the parent RDD, that is, wordsFlatMap (org.apache.spark.OneToOneDependency)
Compute function	To compute the parent and map it to PairRDD
Preferred Location	Ask parent RDD
Partitioner	None

4. Reduce all the values of a given key and sum them up:

```scala
scala> val wordCount = wordsMap.reduceByKey(_+_)
```

The following are the five parts of the `wordCount` RDD:

Part	Description
Partitions	One per reduce task (org.apache.spark.rdd.ShuffledRDDPartition)
Dependencies	Shuffle dependency on each parent (org.apache.spark.ShuffleDependency)
Compute function	To perform additions on shuffled data
Preferred location	None
Partitioner	HashPartitioner (org.apache.spark.HashPartitioner)

This is how an RDD graph of `wordcount` looks at the partition level view:

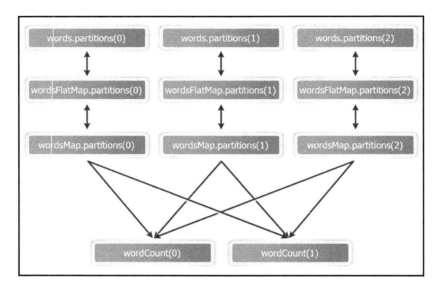

2
Developing Applications with Spark

In this chapter, we will cover the following recipes:

- Exploring the Spark shell
- Developing a Spark applications in Eclipse with Maven
- Developing a Spark applications in Eclipse with SBT
- Developing a Spark application in IntelliJ IDEA with Maven
- Developing a Spark application in IntelliJ IDEA with SBT
- Developing applications using the Zeppelin notebook
- Setting up Kerberos to do authentication
- Enabling Kerberos authentication for Spark

Introduction

Before we start this chapter, it is important that we discuss some trends that directly affect how we develop applications.

Big data applications can be divided into the following three categories:

- Batch
- Interactive
- Streaming or continuous applications

When Hadoop was designed, the primary focus was to provide cost-effective storage for large amounts of data. This remained the main show until it was upended by S3 and other cheaper and more reliable cloud storage alternatives. Compute on this large amounts of data in the Hadoop environment was primarily in the form of MapReduce jobs. Since Spark took the ball from Hadoop (OK! Snatched!) and started running with it, Spark also reflected batch orientation focus in the initial phase, but it did a better job than Hadoop in the case of exploiting in-memory storage.

The most compelling factor of the success of Hadoop was that the cost of storage was hundreds of times lower than traditional data warehouse technologies, such as Teradata.

All these trends were good, but end users still treated it as a sideshow (siloed applications somewhere in the dark alleys of the enterprise) while keeping their low-latency BI/query platforms, running on traditional databases, as the main show. Databases have three decades of head start, so it is understandable that they have optimized the stack to the last bit to improve performance.

During the same time, analytics itself was going through its own transformation. Analytics, which was mostly descriptive (also known as **business intelligence (BI)**/reporting), has evolved into predictive and prescriptive stages. It means that even if Spark had evolved into an engine for traditional BI/dashboarding, it would not have been enough. Spark has notebooks to fill this gap.

Notebooks provide an interactive playground where you can do queries in multiple languages (SQL/Python/Scala). You can run machine learning jobs. You can schedule jobs to be run at a certain time. There are two types of notebooks on the market:

- Open source offerings: Zeppelin and Jupyter
- Commercial XaaS offerings: Databricks Cloud

In this chapter, we will start with the Spark shell, which is a lightweight shell, that this book is focused on. We will also cover a combination of Maven/SBT and Eclipse/IDEA for IDE purposes. In the end, we will explore the notebooks offerings.

Please note that all the commands that run on this shell can run as Scala code bundled as JARs (using `spark-submit` flag). The same code can also be executed on any of the notebooks "as is" without making any changes.

Exploring the Spark shell

Spark comes bundled with a **read–eval–print loop** (**REPL**) shell, which is a wrapper around the Scala shell. Though the Spark shell looks like a command line for simple things, in reality, a lot of complex queries can also be executed using it. A lot of times, the Spark shell is used in the initial development phase and once the code is stabilized, it is written as a class file and bundled as a jar to be run using `spark-submit` flag. This chapter explores different development environments in which Spark applications can be developed.

How to do it...

Hadoop MapReduce's word count, which takes at least three class files and one configuration file, namely **project object model** (**POM**), becomes very simple with the Spark shell. In this recipe, we are going to create a simple one-line text file, upload it to the **Hadoop distributed file system** (**HDFS**), and use Spark to count the occurrences of words. Let's see how:

1. Create the `words` directory using the following command:

   ```
   $ mkdir words
   ```

2. Get into the `words` directory:

   ```
   $ cd words
   ```

3. Create a `sh.txt` text file and enter `"to be or not to be"` in it:

   ```
   $ echo "to be or not to be" > sh.txt
   ```

4. Start the Spark shell:

   ```
   $ spark-shell
   ```

5. Load the `words` directory as RDD:

   ```
   scala> val words =
     sc.textFile("hdfs://localhost:9000/user/hduser/words")
   ```

6. Count the number of lines (result is 1):

   ```
   scala> words.count
   ```

7. Divide the line (or lines) into multiple words and flatten the results:

```
Scala> val wordsFlatMap = words.flatMap(_.split("\\W+"))
```

8. Convert *word* to *(word, 1)*, that is, the output 1 as the value of each occurrence of word as a key (the word or in the sentence has occurred once):

```
Scala> val wordsMap = wordsFlatMap.map( w => (w,1))
```

9. Use the reduceByKey method to add the number of occurrences of each word as a key (the function works on two consecutive values at a time, represented by a and b):

```
Scala> val wordCount = wordsMap.reduceByKey( (a,b) => (a+b))
```

10. Sort the results:

```
Scala> val wordCountSorted = wordCount.sortByKey(true)
```

11. Print the RDD:

```
Scala> wordCountSorted.collect.foreach(println)
```

12. Doing all of the preceding operations in one step is as follows:

```
Scala> sc.textFile("hdfs://localhost:9000/user/hduser/words").
    flatMap(_.split("W+")).map( w => (w,1)). reduceByKey( (a,b)
    => (a+b)).sortByKey(true).collect.foreach(println)
```

13. This gives us the following output:

```
(or,1)
(to,2)
(not,1)
(be,2)
```

There's more...

Now that you have understood the basics, load HDFS with a large amount of text, for example, stories.

If you have the files in a compressed format, you can load them as is in HDFS. Both Hadoop and Spark have codecs for unzipping, which they use based on file extensions.

When `wordsFlatMap` was converted into the `wordsMap` RDD, there was an implicit conversion. This converts the RDD into PairRDD. This is an implicit conversion, which does not require anything to be done. If you are doing it in Scala code, add the following `import` statement:

```
import org.apache.spark.SparkContext._
```

Developing a Spark applications in Eclipse with Maven

Maven as a build tool has become the de-facto standard over the years. It's not surprising if we look a little deeper into what Maven brings. Maven has two primary features and they are:

- **Convention over configuration**: Tools built prior to Maven gave developers the freedom to choose where to put source files, test files, compiled files, and so on. Maven takes away this freedom. Because of this, all the confusion about locations also disappears. In Maven, there is a specific directory structure for everything. The following table shows a few of the most common locations:

`/src/main/scala`	**Source code in Scala**
`/src/main/java`	Source code in Java
`/src/main/resources`	Resources to be used by the source code, such as configuration files
`/src/test/scala`	Test code in Scala
`/src/test/java`	Test code in Java
`/src/test/resources`	Resources to be used by the test code, such as configuration files

- **Declarative dependency management**: In Maven, every library is defined by the following three coordinates:

`groupId`	**A logical way of grouping libraries similar to a package in Java/Scala, which has to be at least the domain name you own, for example,** `org.apache.spark`.
`artifactId`	The name of the project and JAR
`version`	Standard version numbers

In `pom.xml` file (the configuration file that provides Maven all the information about a project), dependencies are declared in the form of these three coordinates. There is no need to search the internet and download, unpack, and copy libraries. All you need to do is provide three coordinates of the dependency JAR you need and Maven will do the rest for you. The following is an example of using a `spark-core` dependency:

```
<dependency>
  <groupId>org.apache.spark</groupId>
  <artifactId>spark-core_2.11</artifactId>
  <version>2.1.0</version>
</dependency>
```

This makes dependency management, including transitive dependencies, very easy. Build tools that came after Maven, such as **simple build tool** (**SBT**) and Gradle, also follow these two rules as is and provide enhancements in other aspects.

Getting ready

From this recipe onward, this chapter assumes you have installed Eclipse. Please visit `http://www.eclipse.org` for details.

How to do it...

Let's see how to install the Maven plugin for Eclipse:

1. Open Eclipse and navigate to **Help | Install New Software**.
2. Click on the **Work with** drop-down menu.
3. Select the **<eclipse version>** update site.
4. Click on **Collaboration tools**.
5. Check **Maven Integration for Eclipse**, as in the following screenshot:

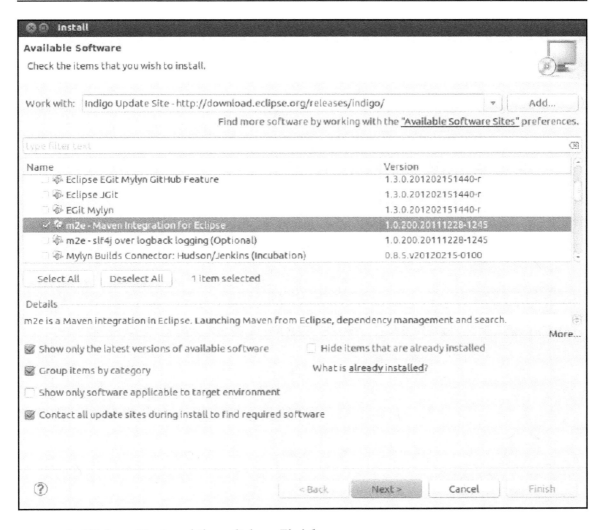

6. Click on **Next** and then click on **Finish**.
7. There will be a prompt to restart Eclipse, and Maven will be installed after the restart.

Now let's see how we can install the Scala plugin for Eclipse:

1. Open Eclipse and navigate to **Help** | **Install New Software**.
2. Click on the **Work with** drop-down menu.
3. Type
   `http://download.scala-ide.org/sdk/helium/e38/scala210/stable/site`.
4. Press **Enter**.
5. Select **Scala IDE for Eclipse**:

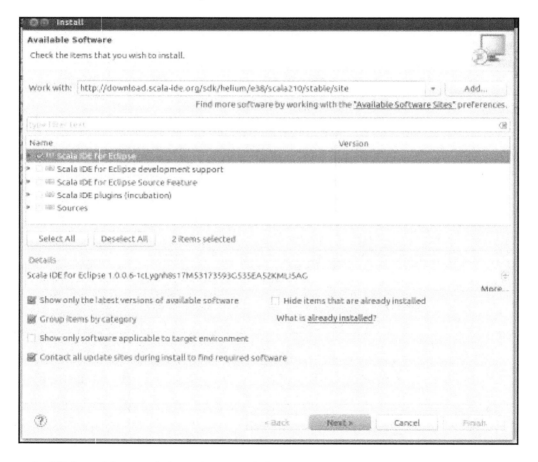

6. Click on **Next** and then click on **Finish**. You will be prompted to restart Eclipse, and Scala will be installed after the restart.
7. Navigate to **Window** | **Open Perspective** | **Scala**.

Eclipse is now ready for Scala development.

Developing a Spark applications in Eclipse with SBT

SBT is a build tool made especially for Scala-based development. SBT follows Maven-based naming conventions and declarative dependency management.

SBT provides the following enhancements over Maven:

- Dependencies are in the form of key-value pairs in the `build.sbt` file, as opposed to the `pom.xml` file in Maven
- It provides a shell that makes it very handy to perform build operations
- For simple projects without dependencies, you do not even need the `build.sbt` file

In the `build.sbt` file, the first line is the project definition:

```
lazy val root = (project in file("."))
```

Each project has an immutable map of key-value pairs. This map is changed by the settings in SBT, as follows:

```
lazy val root = (project in file(".")).
  settings(
    name := "wordcount"
  )
```

Every change in the settings field leads to a new map, as it's an immutable map.

How to do it...

Here's how we go about adding the `sbteclipse` plugin:

1. Add this to the global plugin file:

```
$ mkdir /home/hduser/.sbt/0.13/plugins
$ echo addSbtPlugin("com.typesafe.sbteclipse" % "sbteclipse-plugin"
% "5.1.0" )  > /home/hduser/.sbt/0.13/plugins/plugin.sbt
```

2. Alternatively, you can add the following to your project:

```
$ cd <project-home>
$ echo addSbtPlugin("com.typesafe.sbteclipse" % "sbteclipse-plugin"
% "5.1.0" )  > plugin.sbt
```

3. Start the SBT shell without any arguments:

```
$ sbt
```

4. Type `eclipse` command and it will make an Eclipse-ready project:

```
$ eclipse
```

5. Navigate to **File** | **Import** | **Import existing project into the workspace** to load the project into Eclipse:

Now you can develop the Spark application in Scala using Eclipse and SBT.

Developing a Spark application in IntelliJ IDEA with Maven

IntelliJ IDEA comes bundled with support for Maven. We will see how to create a new Maven project in this recipe.

How to do it...

Perform the following steps to develop a Spark application on IntelliJ IDEA with Maven:

1. Select **Maven** in the new project window and click on **Next**:

2. Enter the three dimensions of the project:

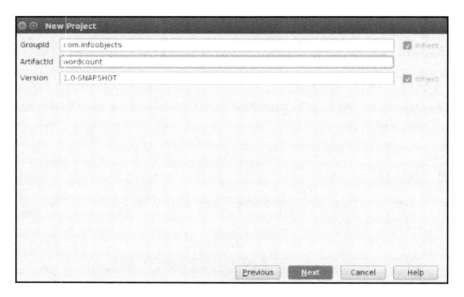

3. Enter the project name and location:

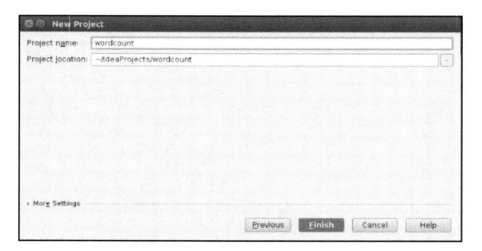

4. Click on **Finish** and the Maven project will be ready.

Developing a Spark application in IntelliJ IDEA with SBT

Before Eclipse became famous, IntelliJ IDEA was considered the best of the breed in IDEs. IDEA has not shed its former glory yet, and a lot of developers love IDEA. IDEA also has a community edition, which is free. It provides native support for SBT, which makes it ideal for SBT and Scala development.

How to do it...

Perform the following steps to develop a Spark application on IntelliJ IDEA with SBT:

1. Add the `sbt-idea` plugin.

2. Add SBT to the global plugin file:

```
$ mkdir /home/hduser/.sbt/0.13/plugins
$ echo addSbtPlugin("com.github.mpeltone" % "sbt-idea" % "1.6.0" )
> /home/hduser/.sbt/0.12/plugins/plugin.sbt
```

3. Alternatively, you can add the SBT plugin to your project as well:

```
$ cd <project-home>
$ echo addSbtPlugin("com.github.mpeltone" % "sbt-idea" % "1.6.0" )
> plugin.sbt
```

IDEA is ready for use with SBT.

Now you can develop the Spark code using Scala and build it using SBT.

Developing applications using the Zeppelin notebook

Apache Zeppelin is a web-based notebook that enables interactive data analytics. In this recipe, we will discuss how to install Zeppelin and the basic developer applications.

How to do it...

1. Download the Zeppelin source code:

   ```
   $ git clone https://github.com/apache/zeppelin.git
   $ cd zeppelin
   ```

2. Explore the archive:

   ```
   $ mvn clean package -DskipTests
   ```

3. Change the directory to conf:

   ```
   $ cd conf
   ```

4. Rename zeppelin-env.sh.template to zeppelin-env.sh:

   ```
   $ mv zeppelin-env.sh.template zeppelin-env.sh
   ```

5. Rename zeppelin-site.xml.template to zeppelin-site.xml:

   ```
   $ mv zeppelin-site.xml.template zeppelin-site.xml
   ```

6. Open zeppelin-env.sh in your favorite editor and change SPARK_HOME to the appropriate value:

   ```
   export SPARK_HOME=/opt/infoobjects/spark
   ```

7. Start Zeppelin:

   ```
   $ bin/zeppelin.sh
   ```

8. Go to `http://localhost:8080` in your web browser and your screen should look like the following:

9. On the top menu, right next to the Zeppelin logo, click on **Notebook** and then on **Create new note**. Select **spark** as the **Default Interpreter**. Enter the **Note Name** as `myfirstnote` (or whatever you would like):

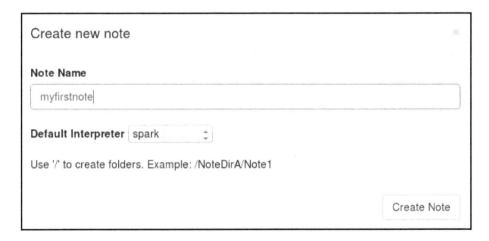

10. Click on **Create Note:**

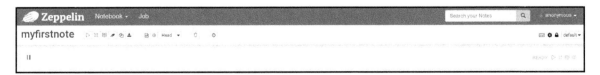

11. Enter the following to get the RDD:

```
val w = sc.textFile("hdfs://localhost:9000/user/hduser/words")
w: org.apache.spark.rdd.RDD[String] = hdfs://localhost:9000/user/hduser/words MapPartitionsRDD[1] at textFile at <console>:27
```

Took 20 sec. Last updated by anonymous at March 12 2017, 7:46:37 PM.

```
w.first
res4: String = to be or not to be
```

Took 1 sec. Last updated by anonymous at March 12 2017, 11:22:57 PM.

Setting up Kerberos to do authentication

User security contains three parts:

- Authentication
- Authorization
- Audit

Authentication simply means verifying who the user claims to be. There are three factors of authentication:

- Who you are
- What you know
- What you have

I am sure you have heard the term *two-factor authentication* everywhere. The more factors you use, the more secure authentication is. More factors also mean more inconvenience; otherwise, three-factor authentication is always used.

Let's understand it with a few examples. Let's say you go to an ATM to withdraw money. How many factors are used? You pull out your ATM card (what you have), insert it, and enter your pin (what you know). This is two-factor authentication.

How about online banking? You enter your username/password (what you know) and you are logged in. So only one factor. This is the reason why for commercial banking, banks give you a mobile token (what you have) using which you get a unique code each time, called **one time password** (**OTP**). These days, banks also send a code to your mobile device via text to enable the second factor of authentication.

Spark uses MIT Kerberos for authentication, like Hadoop. In this recipe, we will learn how to set Kerberos up.

The first step in setting up Kerberos is setting the **key distribution center** (**KDC**). The authentication realm used in this recipe is INFOOBJECTS.COM (please replace it with your value).

How to do it...

1. Making sure /etc/hosts directory reflects the correct **fully qualified domain name** (**FQDN**) (for example, sandbox.infoobjects.com):

   ```
   $ cat /etc/hosts
   ...
   127.0.0.1 localhost infoobjects.com
   ...
   ```

2. Install the admin server:

   ```
   $ sudo apt-get install krb5-kdc krb5-admin-server
   ```

3. During the installation, it would ask for:

   ```
   Default Kerberos version 5 realm: INFOOBJECTS.COM
   Kerberos servers for your realm: infoobjects.com
   Administrative server for your Kerberos realm: infoobjects.com
   ```

4. Check/validate krb5.conf:

   ```
   $ cat /etc/krb5.conf
   ```

5. Configure the Kerberos server. Before you begin, a new realm must be created; this step normally takes a long time. You can use a hack like a random number generator to expedite the process:

```
$ sudo apt-get install rng-tools -y
$ sudo rngd -r /dev/urandom -o /dev/random #not for production
  though
```

6. Create a new realm:

```
$ sudo krb5_newrealm
#enter a master key password and keep it safe or remember it.
```

7. The Kerberos realm is administered using the kadmin utility.
Running admin.local as the root user on KDC allows the administrator to authenticate without having an existing principal. To add a new principal:

```
$ sudo kadmin.local
```

8. Add the **infouser** principal:

```
kadmin.local: addprinc infouser
Enter password for principal "infouser@INFOOBJECTS.COM":
Re-enter password for principal "infouser@INFOOBJECTS.COM":
Principal "infouser@INFOOBJECTS.COM" created.
kadmin.local: quit
```

9. To test the newly created principal, use kinit command. A successful Kerberos setup will return no error if you use the following command:

```
$ kinit infouser@INFOOBJECTS.COM
Password for infouser@INFOOBJECTS.COM:
```

There's more...

Let's understand Kerberos with an example.

Let's say you (client) want to go to a multiplex and watch a movie. It is a special type of multiplex where you may be allowed to watch one movie, two movies, *n* movies, or all the movies depending upon your special ticket. You get this special ticket from a counter outside called **authentication service** (**AS**). Since this special ticket gives you the power to get an actual ticket, let's call it **ticket-granting ticket** (**TGT**).

To get a regular ticket to watch a movie, you need to show TGT to a special counter called **ticket-granting server (TGS)**, and TGS will issue you a ticket (or service ticket). You can present the service ticket to a special movie theater it is valid in and you will be allowed in.

The combination of AS and TGS is called a **key distribution center (KDC)**.

The beauty of TGT is that you do not have to go outside the multiplex, stand in the line, and show your credit card every time.

Kerberos also needs an authentication realm that is simply the domain name fully capitalized. So for `infoobjects.com`, it will be `INFOOBJECTS.COM`. Each server in the Kerberos authentication realm should have an FQDN, for example, `dn5.infoobjects.com`, and it should be forward (FQDN resolving to IP address) and reverse (IP address resolving to FQDN) resolvable.

Enabling Kerberos authentication for Spark

To authenticate against a Kerberos-enabled cluster, the Kerberos configuration needs to be verified first. The configuration can be found in `krb5.conf` file, which includes the locations of KDCs and admin servers of Kerberos's realms of interest, defaults for the current realm and Kerberos applications, and mappings of the host names onto Kerberos's realms.

Check the config file for the correct location of KDC, realm, and so on. You can find this file in the `/etc` directory. Alternatively, you can override the default location by setting the `KRB5_CONFIG` environment variable.

How to do it...

To connect to a Kerberos cluster, you need to use the `keytab` file (pairs of principals and encrypted keys—derived from passwords).

To create a `keytab` file using MIT Kerberos, we will use `ktutil` here. Remember that encryption types (case-sensitive) should be supported and they should be in `krb5.conf`. This is based on the assumption that `infouser@INFOOBJECTS.COM` is there on the Kerberos/respective database. See the following steps to create the `keytab` file for authentication:

1. Add the principal `RC4-HMAC` to the key list:

   ```
   $ ktutil
   ktutil : addent -password -p infouser@INFOOBJECTS.COM -k 1 -e
      RC4-HMAC
   Password for infouser@INFOOBJECTS.COM: [enter your password]
   ```

2. Add the principal `aes256-cts` to the key list:

   ```
   ktutil : addent -password -p infouser@INFOOBJECTS.COM -k 1 -e
      aes256-cts
   Password for infouser@INFOOBJECTS.COM: [enter your password]
   ```

3. Add the principal `aes128-cts` to key list:

   ```
   ktutil : addent -password -p infouser@INFOOBJECTS.COM -k 1 -e
      aes128-cts
   Password for infouser@INFOOBJECTS.COM: [enter your password]
   ```

4. Write the current key list in the Kerberos V5 `keytab` file:

   ```
   ktutil : wkt infouser.keytab
   ktutil : quit
   ```

5. Make sure permissions are correct:

   ```
   $ chmod 600 infouser.keytab
   ```

6. Test whether the generated `keytab` is correct:

   ```
   $ kinit infouser@INFOOBJECTS.COM -k -t infouser.keytab
   ```

7. Now, the `principal` and `keytab` file can be passed with `spark-submit` (with yarn only):

   ```
   spark-submit --keytab "infouser.keytab" --principal
      "infouser@INFOOBJECTS.COM" ...
   ```

8. To do it programmatically, use:

```
UserGroupInformation ugi =
UserGroupInformation.loginUserFromKeytabAndReturnUGI("infouser@INFOOBHECTS.
COM", "infouser.keytab");
        //User principal has maximum life span, so renew accordingly use:
        ugi.reloginFromKeytab(); //as per the need of the application
```

There's more...

Besides user security, another aspect of security is data security. The best way to understand data security is using an example. Let's consider your money is stored in a bank. The bank has to make sure that the money is not only secure while stored in the bank, but also while it is moving between different branches in a van. This brings two types of data security:

- Data security while data is at rest
- Data security while data is in motion or transit

Securing data at rest

Data at rest can be compromised in multiple ways:

- Someone can steal the disks
- Data can be transferred to a different medium

The most popular method is disk-level encryption. This encrypts the whole disk. This is known as the **broad-brush** approach; it is not very efficient, though. The reason being all of the data on the disk does not have the same level of sensitivity. Let's take an example of a customer's data. There is some data which no one, except the authorized user, should ever be able to see, such as **social security number** (**SSN**). There is other information, such as a customer's address, which is still private but is not **personally identifiable information** (**PII**).

 PII is the kind of information that can be used on its own or with other information to identify, contact, or locate a single person.

To encrypt at a finer level of granularity, column level and row level encryption works best. The reliability of encryption also depends upon the algorithm being used. **Advanced encryption standard (AES)** is the default algorithm that comes in two flavors—128 bits and 256 bits—depending upon the size of the encryption keys.

> Encryption is of two types: symmetric encryption and asymmetric encryption. If the same key is used to encrypt and decrypt data, it's called **symmetric encryption**. If different keys are used for encryption and decryption, it's called **asymmetric encryption**. Asymmetric encryption involves a public and private key pair.

Securing data in transit

In simple words, data in transit is secured using a tunnel. The old protocol for the tunnel was **security socket layer (SSL)**, which has been replaced by **transport level security protocol (TLS)**.

3
Spark SQL

Spark SQL is a Spark module for processing structured data. It had a humble start, but now it has become the most important Spark library (as DataFrames/Datasets are replacing RDDs).

This chapter is divided into the following recipes:

- Understanding the evolution of schema awareness
- Understanding the Catalyst optimizer
- Inferring schema using case classes
- Programmatically specifying the schema
- Understanding the Parquet format
- Loading and saving data using the JSON format
- Loading and saving data from relational databases
- Loading and saving data from an arbitrary source
- Understanding joins
- Analyzing nested structures

We will start with a small journey down memory lane to see how schema awareness has slowly evolved into a Spark framework and has now become the core of it. After this, we will discuss how the Catalyst optimizer, the core engine of Spark, works. In the next two recipes, we will focus on converting data from raw format into DataFrames. Then we will discuss how to seamlessly pull and load data into Parquet, JSON, relational, and other formats. Lastly, we will discuss joins and nested structures.

Understanding the evolution of schema awareness

Spark can process data from various data sources, such as HDFS, Cassandra, and relational databases. Big data frameworks (unlike relational database systems) do not enforce a schema while writing data into it. HDFS is a perfect example of where any arbitrary file is welcome during the write phase. The same is true with Amazon S3. Reading data is a different story, however. You need to give some structure to even completely unstructured data to make sense out of it. With this structured data, SQL comes in very handy, when it comes to making sense out of some data.

Getting ready

Spark SQL is a component of the Spark ecosystem, introduced in Spark 1.0 for the first time. It incorporates a project named **Shark**, which was an attempt to make **Hive** run on Spark.

Hive is essentially a relational abstraction; it converts SQL queries into **MapReduce** jobs. See the following figure:

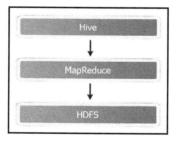

Shark replaced the **MapReduce** part with Spark while retaining most of the code base:

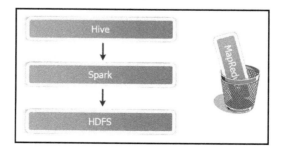

Initially, it worked fine, but very soon, Spark developers hit roadblocks and could not optimize it any further. Finally, they decided to write the SQL engine from scratch, and this gave birth to **Spark SQL**. Refer to the following image for a better understanding:

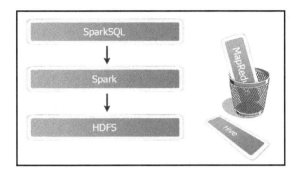

Spark SQL took care of all the performance challenges, but it had to provide compatibility with Hive, and for that reason, a new wrapper context, `HiveContext`, was created on top of `SQLContext`.

Spark SQL supports accessing of data using standard SQL queries and HiveQL, a SQL-like query language that Hive uses. In this chapter, we will explore the different features of Spark SQL. It supports a subset of HiveQL as well as a subset of SQL 92. It runs SQL/HiveQL queries alongside or replaces the existing Hive deployments.

Running SQL is only a part of the reason for the creation of Spark SQL. One big reason is that it helps create and run Spark programs faster. It lets developers to write less code, the program to read less data, and the Catalyst optimizer to do all the heavy lifting.

DataFrames

Spark SQL uses a programming abstraction called **DataFrame**. It is a distributed collection of data, organized in named columns. DataFrame is equivalent to a database table but provides a much finer level of optimization. The DataFrame API also ensures that Spark's performance is consistent across different language bindings.

Let's contrast DataFrames with RDDs. An RDD is an opaque collection of objects with no idea about the format of the underlying data. In contrast, DataFrames have a schema associated with them. You can also look at DataFrames as RDDs with schema added to them. In fact, until Spark 1.2, there was an artifact called **SchemaRDD**, which has now evolved into the DataFrame API. They provide much richer functionality than SchemaRDDs.

This extra information about schema makes it possible for you to do a lot of optimizations, which were not possible otherwise.

DataFrames also transparently load data from various data sources, such as Hive tables, Parquet files, JSON files, and external databases, using JDBC. DataFrames can be viewed as RDDs of row objects that allow users to call procedural Spark APIs, such as a map.

The DataFrame API is available in Scala, Java, Python, and also R, starting from Spark 1.4.

Users can perform relational operations on DataFrames using a **domain-specific language (DSL)**. DataFrames support all the common relational operators, and they take expression objects in a limited DSL that lets Spark capture the structure of the expression.

We will start with the entry point to Spark SQL, that is, SQLContext. We will also cover HiveContext, which is a wrapper around SQLContext to support the Hive functionality. Note that HiveContext is more battle-tested and provides a richer functionality, so it is strongly recommended that you use it even if you do not plan to connect to Hive. Slowly, SQLContext will come to the same level of functionality as HiveContext.

There are two ways to associate the schema with RDDs to create DataFrames. The easy way is to leverage Scala case classes, which we are going to cover first. Spark uses Java reflection to deduce schema from the case classes. There is also a way to programmatically specify the schema for advanced needs, which we will cover next.

Spark SQL provides an easy way to load and save the `Parquet` files, which will also be covered. Lastly, we will cover how to load from and save data to JSON.

Starting from version 2.0 onward, the need to directly call SQLContext or HiveContext has reduced drastically, and most of the functions can now be done by directly dealing with DataFrames.

Datasets

Datasets were added to Spark 1.6 to provide strong typing to DataFrames. In Spark 2.0, Dataset and the DataFrame API were merged to provide one single abstraction. At the bare level, a DataFrame can be considered a Dataset of `Row` objects. This will be enhanced in various places, as you will see in subsequent chapters (for example, in Machine Learning a Dataset of (label, BestVector)).

Datasets provide a rich set of transformation APIs, such as RDDs. It is recommended that you use Datasets as much as possible.

Schema-aware file formats

Having schema-aware building blocks, such as DataFrames, is not enough. It is painful to apply the schema after the fact that is trying to figure out the schema and applying it while reading the data (schema-on-read). The best approach is that schema is embedded with the data when it is stored. This is where schema-aware file formats come into the picture, and this is the reason why they are becoming a standard.

The most popular schema-aware file format in the big data world is Parquet. JSON (the XML killer) is very popular in the web domain. The **Optimized Row Columnar** (**ORC**) format is Hortonworks' and Microsoft's answer to Twitter's and Cloudera's Parquet.

 The primary difference between parquet and ORC is that ORC has indexes, but it does not support nested data. Parquet beautifully handles nested data arbitrarily.

Understanding the Catalyst optimizer

Most of the power of Spark SQL comes from the Catalyst optimizer, so it makes sense to spend some time understanding it. The following diagram shows where exactly the optimization occurs along with the queries:

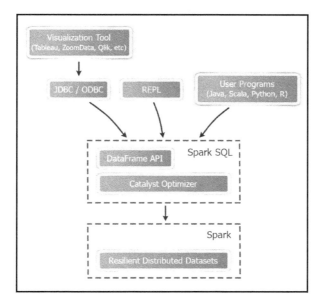

The Catalyst optimizer primarily leverages functional programming constructs of Scala, such as pattern matching. It offers a general framework for transforming trees, which we use to perform analysis, optimization, planning, and runtime code generation.

This optimizer has two primarilly goals:

- To make adding new optimization techniques easy
- To enable external developers to extend the optimizer

Spark SQL uses Catalyst's transformation framework in four phases:

1. Analyzing a logical plan to resolve references.
2. Logical plan optimization.
3. Physical planning.
4. Code generation, to compile the parts of the query to Java byte-code.

Analysis

The analysis phase involves two parts, the first part being:

1. Looking at a SQL query or a DataFrame/Dataset
2. Making sure there are no syntax errors
3. Creating a logical plan out of it
4. This logical plan is still unresolved (as the columns referred to may not exist or may be of a wrong datatype)

The second part of the analysis phase involves:

1. Resolving this plan using the `Catalog` object (which connects to the physical data source)

2. Creating a logical plan, as shown in the following diagram:

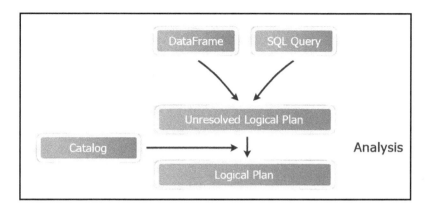

Logical plan optimization

The logical plan optimization phase applies standard rule-based optimizations to the logical plan. These include constant folding, predicate pushdown, projection pruning, null propagation, Boolean expression simplification, and other rules.

I would like to draw special attention to the predicate the pushdown rule here. The concept is simple: if you issue a query in one place to run against some massive data, which is in another place, it can lead to the movement of a lot of unnecessary data across the network.

If we can push down the part of the query where the data is stored and thus filter out unnecessary data, it will reduce network traffic significantly. The following image illustrates this:

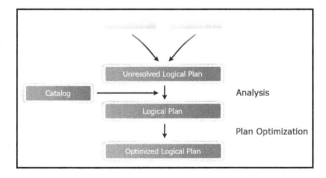

Physical planning

In the **Physical Planning** phase, Spark SQL takes a logical plan and generates one or more physical plans. It then measures the cost of each **Physical Plan** and generates one **Physical Plan** based on it. Refer to the following figure that illustrates this:

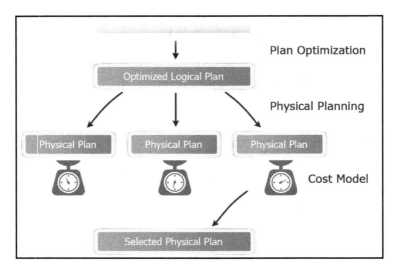

Code generation

The final phase of query optimization involves generating the Java byte-code to run on each machine. It uses a special Scala feature called **Quasi quotes** to accomplish this. The following figure illustrates this:

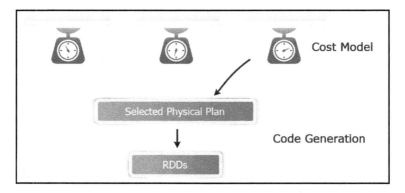

Inferring schema using case classes

In schema-aware formats, such as Parquet and JSON. This is far from the reality, though. A lot of the time data comes in raw format. The next two recipes will cover how to attach a schema to raw data.

In an ideal world, data is stored in schema-aware formats, such as Parquet and JSON. This is far from the reality, though. A lot of the time, data comes in raw format. The next two recipes will cover how to attach a schema to raw data. Case classes are special classes in Scala that provide you with the boilerplate implementation of the constructor, getters (accessors), equals, and hashCode to implement Serializable. Case classes work really well to encapsulate data as objects. Readers familiar with Java, can relate it to **plain old Java objects** (**POJOs**) or Java beans.

The beauty of case classes is that all that grunt work, which is required in Java, can be done with the case classes in a single line of code. Spark uses the reflection feature of the Java programming language on case classes to infer schema.

 Scala is a Java virtual machine based language. What that means is that Scala code compiles to byte-code. This is the reason Spark, which is written in Scala, can seamlessly leverage Java features such as reflection.

How to do it...

1. Start the Spark shell or the Databricks Cloud Scala notebook:

   ```
   $ spark-shell
   ```

2. Create the Person case class:

   ```
   scala> case class Person( first_name:String, last_name:String,
       age:Int)
   ```

3. Load the person directory as a Dataset:

   ```
   scala> val p = spark.read.textFile("s3a://sparkcookbook/person")
   ```

4. Check the first item to kick the tires:

   ```
   scala> p.first
   ```

5. Split each line into an array of strings, based on a comma as the delimiter:

```scala
scala> val pmap = p.map( line => line.split(","))
```

6. Convert the Dataset of Array[String] into the Dataset of `Person` case objects:

```scala
scala> val personDS = pmap.map( p => Person(p(0),p(1),p(2).toInt))
```

7. Register `personDS` as a view:

```scala
scala> personDS.createOrReplaceTempView("person")
```

8. Run a `SQL` query against it:

```scala
scala> val people = spark.sql("select * from person")
```

9. Get the output values from `people`:

```scala
scala> people.show
```

There's more...

This recipe was about learning how to use case classes to attach schema and the input data we used here is in `CSV` format. Also, there is another way to load data:

```scala
scala> val people =
spark.read.format("csv").load("s3a://sparkcookbook/person")
```

The output looks like this:

```
+------+-------+---+
| _c0| _c1| _c2|
+------+-------+---+
|Barack| Obama| 55|
|George| Bush| 70|
| Bill|Clinton| 70|
+------+-------+---+
```

Now there are two ways to fix this. The first approach is to supply custom column names, such as the following:

```scala
scala> val people =
spark.read.format("csv").load("s3a://sparkcookbook/person").select($"_c0".a
s("first_name"),$"_c1".as("last_name"),$"_c2".as("age").cast("Int"))
```

The second way is to load data that already has column headers, such as the following:

```
scala> val p =
spark.read.format("csv").option("header","true").load("s3a://sparkcookbook/
people")
```

Let's see how the schema looks:

```
scala> p.printSchema
root
 |-- First Name: string (nullable = true)
 |-- Last Name: string (nullable = true)
 |-- Age: string (nullable = true)
```

So, it did the job but not as we expected. We expected Age to be an integer. So let's fix this issue:

```
val p =
spark.read.format("csv").option("header","true").option("inferschema","true
").load("s3a://sparkcookbook/people")
```

What if the data is not in CSV but separated by some other delimiter? Let's redo the previous command by treating the comma as a general delimiter:

```
val p =
spark.read.option("delimiter",",").option("header","true").option("infersch
ema","true").csv("s3a://sparkcookbook/people")
```

Programmatically specifying the schema

There are a few cases where case classes might not work; one of these cases is where case classes cannot take more than 22 fields. Another case can be that you do not know about the schema beforehand. In this approach, data is loaded as an RDD of the Row objects. The schema is created separately using the StructType and StructField objects, which represent a table and a field, respectively. The schema is applied to the Row RDD to create a DataFrame.

How to do it...

1. Start the Spark shell or Databricks Cloud Scala notebook:

   ```
   $ spark-shell
   ```

2. Import the Spark SQL datatypes and `Row` objects:

    ```scala
    scala> import org.apache.spark.sql._
    scala> import org.apache.spark.sql.types._
    ```

3. Create the schema using the `StructType` and `StructField` objects. The `StructField` object takes parameters in the form of param name, param type, and nullability:

    ```scala
    scala> val schema = StructType(
    Array(StructField("first_name",StringType,true),
    StructField("last_name",StringType,true),
    StructField("age",IntegerType,true)
    ))
    ```

4. Load the `person` data in a Dataset and attach the schema to it:

    ```scala
    scala> val personDS =
    spark.read.schema(schema).csv("s3a://sparkcookbook/person")
    ```

5. Register `personDS` as a view:

    ```scala
    scala> personDS.createOrReplaceTempView("person")
    ```

6. Run a `SQL` query against it:

    ```scala
    scala> val persons = spark.sql("select * from person")
    ```

7. Get the output values from `persons`:

    ```scala
    scala> persons.show
    ```

In this recipe, you learned how to create a DataFrame by programmatically specifying the schema.

How it works...

A `StructType` object defines the schema. You can consider it equivalent to a table or a row in the relational world. `StructType` takes in an array of the `StructField` objects, as in the following signature:

```scala
StructType(fields: Array[StructField])
```

A `StructField` object has the following signature:

```
StructField(name: String, dataType: DataType, nullable: Boolean = true,
metadata: Metadata = Metadata.empty)
```

Here is some more information on the parameters used:

- `name`: This represents the name of the field.
- `dataType`: This shows the datatype of the field.
- The following datatypes are allowed:
  - `IntegerType`
  - `FloatType`
  - `BooleanType`
  - `ShortType`
  - `LongType`
  - `ByteType`
  - `DoubleType`
  - `StringType`

- `nullable`: This shows whether the field can be null.
- `metadata`: This shows the metadata of the field. Metadata is a wrapper over Map (String, Any) so that it can contain any arbitrary metadata.

Understanding the Parquet format

the Google Dremel paper. In Parquet, data in a single column is stored contiguously.

Apache Parquet is a columnar data storage format, specifically designed for big data storage and processing. It is based on record shredding and the assembly algorithm from the Google Dremel paper. In Parquet, data in a single column is stored contiguously. The columnar format gives Parquet some unique benefits. For example, if you have a table with 100 columns and you mostly access 10 columns in a row-based format, you will have to load all the 100 columns, as the granularity level is at the row level. But, in Parquet, you will only need to load 10 columns. Another benefit is that since all of the data in a given column is of the same datatype (by definition), compression is much more efficient.

While we are discussing Parquet and its merits, it's a good idea to discuss the economic reason behind Parquet's success. There are two factors that every practitioner would like to drive down to zero, and they are latency and cost. In short, we all want fast query speeds at the least cost possible. General-purpose stores, such as Amazon S3 and HDFS, are as cheap as it can get. So the question arises: how to bring these new data storage systems to the same level of performance as seen in traditional database systems. This is where Parquet comes to the rescue. Parquet is very popular but is not the only shining star there when it comes to ad hoc query processing, especially on a public cloud. Facebook-born Presto on S3 is gaining a lot of traction and is worth paying attention to. In fact, AWS released a new service called Athena, which runs on this combo.

How to do it...

1. Start the Spark shell or Scala notebook in the Databricks Cloud:

   ```
   $ spark-shell
   ```

2. Create a case class for `Person`:

   ```
   scala> case class Person(firstName: String, lastName: String,
     age:Int)
   ```

3. Load the `person` data as a DataSet and map it to the `Person` case class:

   ```
   scala> val personDS =
     spark.read.textFile("s3a://sparkcookbook/person").map( line =>
     line.split(",")).map( p => Person(p(0),p(1),p(2).toInt))
   ```

4. Register the `person` DataSet as a `temp` table so that SQL queries can be run against it. Note that the DataFrame name does not have to be the same as the table name:

   ```
   scala> person.createOrReplaceTempView("person")
   ```

5. Select all `persons` whose age is over `60` years:

   ```
   scala> val sixtyPlus = spark.sql("select * from person where
     age > 60")
   ```

6. Print the values:

   ```
   scala> sixtyPlus.show
   ```

7. Save this `sixtyPlus` DataFrame in the `Parquet` format:

```scala
scala> sixtyPlus.write.parquet(
  "hdfs://localhost:9000/user/hduser/sp.parquet")
```

> **TIP**
>
> What if you would like to write data in a compressed format, for example, snappy? Use the following code:
> `sixtyPlus.write.option("compression","snappy").parquet("hdfs://localhost:9000/user/hduser/sp.parquet")`

8. The previous step created a directory called `sp.parquet` in the HDFS root. You can run the `hdfs dfs -ls` command in another shell to make sure that it's created:

```
$ hdfs dfs -ls sp.parquet
```

9. Load the contents of the `Parquet` files in the Spark shell:

```scala
scala> val parquetDF = spark.read.parquet
  ("hdfs://localhost:9000/user/hduser/sp.parquet")
```

10. Register the loaded `Parquet` DataFrame as a `temp` view:

```scala
scala> parquetRDD.createOrReplaceTempView("sixty_plus")
```

11. Run a query against the preceding `temp` view:

```scala
scala> spark.sql("select * from sixty_plus")
```

How it works...

Let's spend some time understanding the Parquet format at a deeper level. The following is some sample data represented in a table format:

First_Name	Last_Name	Age
Barack	Obama	55
George	Bush	70
Bill	Clinton	70

In the row format, the data will be stored like this:

Barack	Obama	55	George	Bush	70	Bill	Clinton	70

In the columnar layout, the data will be stored like this:

Barack	George	Bill	Obama	Bush	Clinton	56	70	70

The following diagram illustrates how the data is laid out in a file:

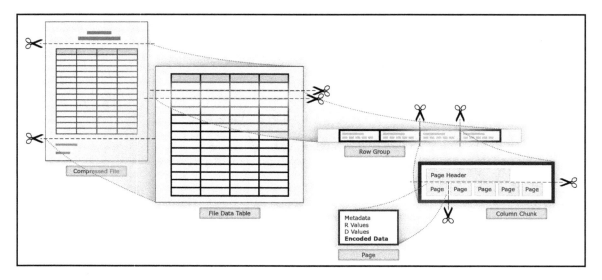

Here's a brief description of the different parts:

- **Row group**: This shows the horizontal partitioning of the data into rows. A row group consists of column chunks.
- **Column chunk**: A column chunk has data for a given column in a row group. A column chunk is always physically contiguous. A row group has only one column chunk per column.
- **Page header**: Every column chunk has a shared page header.
- **Page**: A column chunk is divided into pages. A page is a unit of storage and cannot be further divided. Pages are written back to back in a column chunk. The data on a page can be compressed.

If a column has null values, it's not stored. If a column chunk has null values, even the column chunk is not stored.

Data in Parquet is not only compressed but also encoded. This leads to a significant reduction in disk footprint, network I/O footprint, and memory footprint. There is a slight increase in CPU cycles as data needs to be compressed/decompressed and encoded/decoded.

Partitioning

Parquet has built-in support for partitioning. This works great when you need to partition data by selecting a column, for example, by year, month, date, or hour. The flip side is that it makes ad hoc queries slow.

Predicate pushdown

Parquet only pulls data that is filtered for a row group, column chunks, and select partitions. This makes queries both fast and light. A natural question that comes to mind is: what is the big deal about it, every database does it? The big deal is that Parquet is not a database, just a file format--files that can be stored in a regular store, such as HDFS or S3.

Parquet Hive interoperability

If there is already some data in a Hive table, say, the `person` table, you can directly save it in the `Parquet` format by performing the following steps:

1. Create a table named `person_parquet` with the schema, the same as `person`, but in the Parquet storage format (for Hive 0.13 onward):

   ```
   hive> create table person_parquet like person stored as parquet
   ```

2. Insert data in the `person_parquet` table by importing it from the `person` table:

   ```
   hive> insert overwrite table person_parquet select * from person;
   ```

3. Sometimes, data imported from other sources, such as Impala, saves the string in the binary form. To convert it into a string while reading, set the following property in `SparkConf`, as shown in the following code:

   ```
   scala> spark.setConf("spark.sql.parquet.binaryAsString","true")
   ```

Loading and saving data using the JSON format

JSON is a lightweight data-interchange format. It is based on a subset of the JavaScript programming language. JSON's popularity is directly related to XML getting unpopular. XML was a great solution to provide a structure to the data in plain text format. With time, XML documents became heavier, and the overhead was not worth it.

JSON solved this problem by providing a structure with minimal overhead. Some people call JSON **fat-free XML**.

JSON's syntax follows these rules:

- Data is in the form of key-value pairs:

    ```
    "firstName" : "Bill"
    ```

- There are four datatypes in JSON:
    - String ("firstName" : "Barack")
    - Number ("age" : 56)
    - Boolean ("alive": true)
    - null ("manager" : null)
- Data is delimited by commas
- Curly braces { } represents an object:

    ```
    { "firstName" : "Bill", "lastName": "Clinton", "age": 70 }
    ```

- Square brackets [] represent an array:

    ```
    [{ "firstName" : "Bill", "lastName": "Clinton", "age": 70 }
      {"firstName": "Barack","lastName": "Obama", "age": 55}]
    ```

In this recipe, we will explore how to save and load data in the JSON format.

How to do it...

1. Open the terminal and create the `person` data in the JSON format:

```
        $ mkdir jsondata
$ vi jsondata/person.json
{"first_name" : "Barack", "last_name" : "Obama", "age" : 55}
{"first_name" : "George", "last_name" : "Bush", "age" : 70 }
{"first_name" : "Bill", "last_name" : "Clinton", "age" : 70 }
```

2. Upload the `jsondata` directory to HDFS:

```
    $ hdfs dfs -put jsondata /user/hduser/jsondata
```

3. Start the `spark-shell`:

```
    $ spark-shell
```

4. Load the `jsondata` directory from HDFS:

```
    scala> val person = spark.read.json
        ("hdfs://localhost:9000/user/hduser/jsondata")
```

5. Register the `person` **DataFrame** (**DF**) as a `temp` table so that the SQL queries can be run against it:

```
    scala> jsondata.createOrReplaceTempView("person")
```

6. Select all the persons whose age is over 60 years:

```
    scala> val sixtyPlus = spark.sql("select * from person where
        age > 60")
```

7. Print the values:

```
    scala> sixtyPlus.show
```

8. Let's save this `sixtyPlus` DF in the JSON format:

```
    scala> sixtyPlus.write.format("json").save
        ("hdfs://localhost:9000/user/hduser/sp")
```

9. In the last step, you created a directory called `sp` in the HDFS root. You can run the `hdfs dfs -ls` command in another shell to make sure it's created:

```
    $ hdfs dfs -ls sp
```

How it works...

The `spark.read.json` internally uses `TextInputFormat`, which processes one line at a time. Therefore, one JSON record cannot be on multiple lines. It would be a valid JSON format if you use multiple lines, but it will not work with Spark and will throw an exception.

It is allowed to have more than one object in a line. For example, you can have the information of two persons in one line as an array, as follows:

```
[{"firstName":"Barack", "lastName":"Obama"},{"firstName":"Bill",
"lastName":"Clinton"}]
```

This recipe concludes the saving and loading of data in the JSON format using Spark.

Loading and saving data from relational databases

Loading data into Spark from relational databases is very common. As the Spark-based big data lake is becoming a replacement for traditional Enterprise Data warehouses, Spark needs to connect to support for JDBC.

Getting ready

Make sure that the JDBC driver JAR is visible on the client node and all the slave nodes on which the executor will run.

How to do it...

1. Create a table named `person` in MySQL using the following DDL:

```
CREATE TABLE 'person' (
  'person_id' int(11) NOT NULL AUTO_INCREMENT,
  'first_name' varchar(30) DEFAULT NULL,
  'last_name' varchar(30) DEFAULT NULL,
  'gender' char(1) DEFAULT NULL,
  'age' tinyint(4) DEFAULT NULL,
  PRIMARY KEY ('person_id')
)
```

2. Insert some data:

```
Insert into person values('Barack','Obama','M',55);
Insert into person values('Bill','Clinton','M',70);
Insert into person values('Hillary','Clinton','F',69);
Insert into person values('Bill','Gates','M',61);
Insert into person values('Michelle','Obama','F',52);
```

3. Download `mysql-connector-java-x.x.xx-bin.jar` from `http://dev.mysql.com/downloads/connector/j/`.

4. Make the MySQL driver available to the `spark-shell` and launch it:

```
$ spark-shell --driver-class-path/path-to-mysql-jar/mysql-
   connector-java-5.1.34-bin.jar
```

 Note that `path-to-mysql-jar` is not the actual path name. You need to use your pathname. This is just a syntax.

5. Construct a JDBC URL:

```
scala> val url="jdbc:mysql://localhost:3306/hadoopdb"
```

6. Create a connection properties object with a username and password:

```
scala> val prop = new java.util.Properties
scala> prop.setProperty("user","hduser")
scala> prop.setProperty("password","********")
```

7. Load the DataFrame with the JDBC data source (`url`, `table name`, and `properties`):

```
scala> val people = sqlContext.read.jdbc(url,"person",prop)
```

8. Show the results in a nice tabular format by executing the following command:

```
scala> people.show
```

9. This has loaded the whole table. What if I would like to only load males (url, table name, predicates, and properties)? To do this, run the following command:

```
scala> val males = spark.read.jdbc
       (url,"person",Array("gender='M'"),prop)
scala> males.show
```

10. Show only the first names by executing the following command:

```
scala> val first_names = people.select("first_name")
scala> first_names.show
```

11. Show only people below 60 years of age by executing the following command:

```
scala> val below60 = people.filter(people("age") < 60)
scala> below60.show
```

12. Group people by gender as follows:

```
scala> val grouped = people.groupBy("gender")
```

13. Find the number of males and females by executing the following command:

```
scala> val gender_count = grouped.count
scala> gender_count.show
```

14. Find the average age of males and females by executing the following command:

```
scala> val avg_age = grouped.avg("age")
scala> avg_age.show
```

15. Now if you'd like to save this avg_age data to a new table, run the following command:

```
scala> gender_count.write.jdbc(url,"gender_count",prop)
```

16. Save the people DataFrame in the Parquet format:

```
scala> people.write.parquet("people.parquet")
```

17. Save the people DataFrame in the JSON format:

```
scala> people.write.json("people.json")
```

Loading and saving data from an arbitrary source

So far, we have covered five data sources that are built-in with DataFrames: `Parquet` (default), `text`, `json`, `csv`, and `jdbc`. DataFrames are not limited to these five and can load and save to any arbitrary data source by specifying the format manually.

In this recipe, we will cover the loading and saving of data from arbitrary sources.

How to do it...

1. Start the Spark shell:

   ```
   $ spark-shell
   ```

2. Load the data from Parquet; since `parquet` is the default data source, you do not have to specify it:

   ```
   scala> val people = spark.read.load("hdfs://localhost:
      9000/user/hduser/people.parquet")
   ```

3. Load the data from `parquet` by manually specifying the format:

   ```
   scala> val people = spark.read.format("parquet").load
      ("hdfs://localhost:9000/user/hduser/people.parquet")
   ```

4. For inbuilt datatypes, you do not have to specify the full format name; only specifying "`parquet`", "`json`", or "`jdbc`" would work:

   ```
   scala> val people = spark.read.format("parquet").load
      ("hdfs://localhost:9000/user/hduser/people.parquet")
   ```

    When writing data, there are four save modes: `append`, `overwrite`, `errorIfExists`, and `ignore`. The `append` mode adds data to a data source, `overwrite` overwrites it, `errorIfExists` throws an exception that the data already exists, and `ignore` does nothing when the data already exists.

5. Save people as JSON in the `append` mode:

   ```
   scala> val people = people.write.format("json").mode
   ("append").save ("hdfs://localhost:9000/user/hduser/people.json")
   ```

There's more...

The Spark SQL's data source API saves to a variety of data sources. For more information, visit http://spark-packages.org/.

Understanding joins

A SQL join is a process of combining two datasets based on a common column. Joins come in really handy for extracting extra values by combining multiple tables.

Getting ready

We are going to use **Yelp** data as part of this recipe, which is provided by Yelp for Yelp Data Challenge. The data is divided into the following six files:

- yelp_academic_dataset_business.json
- yelp_academic_dataset_review.json
- yelp_academic_dataset_user.json
- yelp_academic_dataset_checkin.json
- yelp_academic_dataset_tip.json
- photos (from the photos auxiliary file)

We are going to use this data for multiple purposes across the book. This data really works for this recipe as it has joins everywhere.

This data is already loaded in the s3a://sparkcookbook/yelpdata Amazon S3 bucket for your convenience. Spark provides a convenient way to access S3 using the s3a prefix. This is not the standard way to access S3 buckets though. S3 buckets are accessed using HTTP URL. There are a few ways to specify the URL. For example, in the case of the sparkcookbook bucket, the following options are valid:
http://sparkcookbook.s3.amazonaws.com and http://s3.amazonaws.com/sparkcookbook.

How to do it...

1. Start the Spark shell or Databricks Cloud Scala notebook:

   ```
   $ spark-shell
   ```

2. Load business data as a DataFrame:

   ```
   scala> val businesses = spark.read.format("json").load
     ("s3a://sparkcookbook/yelpdata/
        yelp_academic_dataset_business.json")
   ```

3. Print the schema:

   ```
   scala> businesses.printSchema
    root
    |-- address: string (nullable = true)
    |-- attributes: array (nullable = true)
    |  |-- element: string (containsNull = true)
    |-- business_id: string (nullable = true)
    |-- categories: array (nullable = true)
    |  |-- element: string (containsNull = true)
    |-- city: string (nullable = true)
    |-- hours: array (nullable = true)
    |  |-- element: string (containsNull = true)
    |-- is_open: long (nullable = true)
    |-- latitude: double (nullable = true)
    |-- longitude: double (nullable = true)
    |-- name: string (nullable = true)
    |-- neighborhood: string (nullable = true)
    |-- postal_code: string (nullable = true)
    |-- review_count: long (nullable = true)
    |-- stars: double (nullable = true)
    |-- state: string (nullable = true)
    |-- type: string (nullable = true)
   ```

4. Do the count:

   ```
   scala> businesses.count
   Long = 144072
   ```

The size of the dataset helps us determine the **join** strategy. Here's an example: if one data size is significantly smaller than the other, we can use the broadcast join.

5. Load reviews as a DataFrame:

```scala
scala> val reviews = spark.read.format("json").load
  ("s3a://sparkcookbook/yelpdata/
    yelp_academic_dataset_review.json")
```

6. Print the schema:

```scala
scala> reviews.printSchema
 root
 |-- business_id: string (nullable = true)
 |-- cool: long (nullable = true)
 |-- date: string (nullable = true)
 |-- funny: long (nullable = true)
 |-- review_id: string (nullable = true)
 |-- stars: long (nullable = true)
 |-- text: string (nullable = true)
 |-- type: string (nullable = true)
 |-- useful: long (nullable = true)
 |-- user_id: string (nullable = true)
```

7. Count the number of reviews:

```scala
scala> reviews.count
 Long = 4153150
```

8. Load users as a DataFrame:

```scala
scala> val users = spark.read.format("json").load
  ("s3a://sparkcookbook/yelpdata/
    yelp_academic_dataset_user.json")
```

9. Print the schema:

```scala
scala> users.printSchema
 root
 |-- average_stars: double (nullable = true)
 |-- compliment_cool: long (nullable = true)
 |-- compliment_cute: long (nullable = true)
 |-- compliment_funny: long (nullable = true)
 |-- compliment_hot: long (nullable = true)
 |-- compliment_list: long (nullable = true)
 |-- compliment_more: long (nullable = true)
 |-- compliment_note: long (nullable = true)
 |-- compliment_photos: long (nullable = true)
 |-- compliment_plain: long (nullable = true)
 |-- compliment_profile: long (nullable = true)
 |-- compliment_writer: long (nullable = true)
```

```
|-- cool: long (nullable = true)
|-- elite: array (nullable = true)
|  |-- element: string (containsNull = true)
|-- fans: long (nullable = true)
|-- friends: array (nullable = true)
|  |-- element: string (containsNull = true)
|-- funny: long (nullable = true)
|-- name: string (nullable = true)
|-- review_count: long (nullable = true)
|-- type: string (nullable = true)
|-- useful: long (nullable = true)
|-- user_id: string (nullable = true)
|-- yelping_since: string (nullable = true)
```

10. Count the number of users:

```
scala> users.count
   Long = 1029432
```

11. Load tips as a DataFrame:

```
scala> val tips = spark.read.format("json").load
   ("s3a://sparkcookbook/yelpdata/
      yelp_academic_dataset_tip.json")
```

12. Print the schema:

```
scala> tips.printSchema
root
|-- business_id: string (nullable = true)
|-- date: string (nullable = true)
|-- likes: long (nullable = true)
|-- text: string (nullable = true)
|-- type: string (nullable = true)
|-- user_id: string (nullable = true)
```

13. Count the `tips`:

```
scala> tips.count
Long = 946600
```

14. Load reviews and tips as temporary views:

```
scala> reviews.createOrReplaceTempView("reviews")
scala> tips.createOrReplaceTempView("tips")
```

15. Do a Shuffle hash join on reviews and tips:

```scala
scala> val reviews_tips = spark.sql("select * FROM reviews JOIN
    tips ON reviews.user_id = tips.user_id and
        reviews.business_id = tips.business_id")
```

16. Do a count on `reviews_tips`:

```scala
scala> reviews_tips.count
Long = 372288
```

This count is much lower than the individual DataFrame count in reviews and tips, and the reason behind this is that the businesses for which the user has provided tips need not be the same as the businesses for which reviews are written.

17. What if we would like all the reviews, regardless of whether they have associated tips or not:

```scala
scala> val all_reviews_tips = spark.sql("select * FROM reviews
    LEFT JOIN tips ON reviews.user_id = tips.user_id and
        reviews.business_id = tips.business_id")
```

How it works...

There are primarily three types of joins in Spark:

- Shuffle hash join (default)
- Broadcast hash join
- Cartesian join

Shuffle hash join

The Shuffle hash join is the most basic type of join and is derived from the joins in MapReduce. Let's say we would like to join the review data and tip data for every user. A Shuffle hash join will go through the following steps:

1. Map through the review DataFrame using `user_id`, `business_id` as a key.
2. Map through the tip DataFrame using `user_id`, `business_id` as a key.
3. Shuffle review data by `user_id`, `business_id`.
4. Shuffle tip data by `user_id`, `business_id`.

5. Join both the datasets using the reduce phase. Data with the same keys will be on the same machine and sorted.

As in MapReduce, the Shuffle hash join works best when data is not skewed and evenly distributed among the keys.

Broadcast hash join

The easiest optimization is that if one of the datasets is small enough to fit in memory, it should be broadcasted to every compute node. This use case is very common as data needs to be combined with side data, such as a dictionary, all the time.

Mostly joins are slow due to too much data being shuffled over the network. With the Broadcast join, the smaller dataset is copied to all the worker nodes so the original parallelism of the larger DataFrame is maintained.

The cartesian join

Cartesian join happens when every row of one DataFrame is joined with every row of the other DataFrame. This can explode the number of rows very fast. Two DataFrames, each with a modest 100 K rows, can result in 10 billion rows with a cartesian join.

There's more...

You can also check which execution strategy is being used using `explain`:

```
scala> mydf.explain
scala> mydf.queryExecution.executedPlan
```

Analyzing nested structures

There is a reason why the nested structures recipe is right after that of joins. Nested structures have traditionally been associated with web-based applications and hyper-scale companies. The most common format of nested structures is JSON. JSON inherited nested structures from XML, which JSON made irrelevant.

Getting ready

The power of nested structures goes far beyond traditional use cases, though. It has been very difficult to represent hierarchical data in highly normalized databases. Data needs to be joined across tables as needed. This does provide us with flexibility. Let's understand it with the example we covered in the previous recipe. In the Yelp dataset, a user reviews a business, which is represented by `yelp_academic_dataset_review.json`. In reality, a user reviews multiple businesses and a business is reviewed by multiple users. One would argue that it represents standard *NxN* relationships between entities, so what's the big deal here? The challenges come in how distributed systems operate. To make a join happen, the data needs to be shuffled over the network, which is very costly.

A high degree of normalization definitely saves us some disk space and minimizes redundancy, but in the big data world, both are not real issues. The real issue is latency. The question that arises is: how should we represent nested data? Should users be nested inside businesses or businesses under users? There is no perfect answer here as it depends on what your query is. If you would like to query both ways, you'll need two nested structures. Once the structure is created, we can retain default parallelism at the node level, and no shuffle is required.

One question that arises is: how are nested structures different than denormalized data structures? The difference is that the amount of data stored is much less, which leads to efficiencies.

How to do it...

1. Start the Spark shell or Databricks Cloud Scala notebook:

   ```
   $ spark-shell
   ```

2. Load the reviews as a DataFrame:

   ```scala
   scala> val reviews = spark.read.format("json").option
     ("inferschema","true").load("s3a://sparkcookbook/yelpdata/
       yelp_academic_dataset_review.json").withColumn("rtype",
         ($"type")).drop("type")
   ```

3. Print the schema:

   ```scala
   scala> reviews.printSchema
   root
    |-- business_id: string (nullable = true)
   ```

```
|-- cool: long (nullable = true)
|-- date: string (nullable = true)
|-- funny: long (nullable = true)
|-- review_id: string (nullable = true)
|-- stars: long (nullable = true)
|-- text: string (nullable = true)
|-- useful: long (nullable = true)
|-- user_id: string (nullable = true)
|-- rtype: string (nullable = true)
```

4. Create the `Review` case class:

```
scala> case class Review(business_id:String,cool:Long,date:
    String,funny:Long,review_id:String,stars:
        Long,text:String,rtype:String,useful:Long,user_id:String)
```

5. Convert the `review` DF into a DataSet:

```
scala> val reviewsDS = reviews.as[Review]
```

6. Create the `BusinessReviews` case class to represent all the reviews for a given business:

```
scala> case class BusinessReviews(business_id:String,
    reviews:List[Review])
```

7. Create the `nesting` function:

```
scala> val nestingFunction = (key: String, iter:
    Iterator[Review]) => BusinessReviews(business_id=key,
        reviews=iter.toList)
```

8. Group reviews by `business_id` and convert it into a nested format:

```
scala> val nestedreviews = reviewDS.groupByKey(_.business_id)
    .mapGroups((key,iter) => nestingFunction(key,iter))
```

9. Save `nestedreviews` to the s3 bucket (change it to the appropriate bucket, otherwise the following command will fail):

```
scala> nestedreviews.write.json("s3a://io.playground/nested")
```

10. Load the bucket:

```
scala> val r = spark.read.format("json").load
    ("s3a://io.playground/nested")
```

11. Print the schema:

```scala
scala> r.printSchema
root
 |-- business_id: string (nullable = true)
 |-- reviews: array (nullable = true)
 |    |-- element: struct (containsNull = true)
 |    |    |-- business_id: string (nullable = true)
 |    |    |-- cool: long (nullable = true)
 |    |    |-- date: string (nullable = true)
 |    |    |-- funny: long (nullable = true)
 |    |    |-- review_id: string (nullable = true)
 |    |    |-- rtype: string (nullable = true)
 |    |    |-- stars: long (nullable = true)
 |    |    |-- text: string (nullable = true)
 |    |    |-- useful: long (nullable = true)
 |    |    |-- user_id: string (nullable = true)
```

12. Import SQL functions, such as explode:

```scala
scala> import org.apache.spark.sql.functions._
```

13. Use the explode function so that business_id is repeated for every review:

```scala
scala> val exploded = n.select($"business_id",
  explode($"reviews"))
```

14. Display the exploded DataFrame:

```scala
scala> display(exploded)
```

4
Working with External Data Sources

Apache Spark depends upon the big data pipeline to get data. The pipeline starts with source systems. The source system data ingress can be arbitrarily complex due to the following reasons:

- Nature of the data (relational, non-relational)
- Data being dirty (yes, it's more of a rule than exception)
- Source data being at a different level of normalization (SAP data, for example, has an extremely high degree of normalization)
- Lack of consistency in the data (data needs to be harmonized so that it speaks the same language)

In this chapter, we will explore how Apache Spark connects to various data sources. This chapter is divided into the following recipes:

- Loading data from the local filesystem
- Loading data from HDFS
- Loading data from Amazon S3
- Loading data from Apache Cassandra

Introduction

Spark provides a unified runtime for big data. **Hadoop Distributed File System** (**HDFS**) has traditionally been the most used storage platform for Spark as it has provided the most cost-effective storage for unstructured and semi-structured data on commodity hardware. This has been upended by public cloud storage systems, especially Amazon S3. This edition of the book reflects that reality with special emphasis on connectivity to S3.

That being said, Spark exclusively leverages Hadoop's `InputFormat` and `OutputFormat` interfaces. `InputFormat` is responsible for creating `InputSplits` from input data and dividing it further into records. `OutputFormat` is responsible for writing to storage. Following image illustrates InputFormat metaphorically:

We will start by writing to the local filesystem and then move over to loading data from HDFS. In the *Loading data from HDFS* recipe, we will cover the most common file format: regular text files. We will also explore loading data stored in Amazon S3, a leading cloud storage platform. Finally, we will explore loading data from Apache Cassandra, which is a NoSQL database.

Loading data from the local filesystem

Though the local filesystem is not a good fit to store big data due to disk size limitations and lack of distributed nature, technically you can load data in distributed systems using the local filesystem. But then the file/directory you are accessing has to be available on each node.

Please note that if you are planning to use this feature to load side data, it is not a good idea. To load side data, Spark has a broadcast variable feature, which will be discussed in upcoming chapters.
Enriching data with side data is a very common use-case and we will cover how to do it in the subsequent chapters.

In this recipe, we will look at how to load data in Spark from the local filesystem.

How to do it...

Let's start with the example of Shakespeare's `"to be or not to be"`:

1. Create the `words` directory by using the following command:

   ```
   $ mkdir words
   ```

2. Get into the `words` directory:

   ```
   $ cd words
   ```

3. Create the `sh.txt` text file and enter `"to be or not to be"` in it:

   ```
   $ echo "to be or not to be" > sh.txt
   ```

4. Start the Spark shell:

   ```
   $ spark-shell
   ```

5. Load the `words` directory as a DataFrame:

   ```
   scala> val wdf = spark.read.text("file:///home/hduser/words")
   ```

6. Convert `wdf` dataset into a dataset of strings `wds` :

   ```
   scala> val wds = wdf.as[String]
   ```

It is very important to convert a DataFrame into a dataset before doing operations, which were done by RDDs in the past. DataFrame, essentially, is a collection of rows, and converting it into a more meaningful data type usually helps. There is also an easier way: `val wds = spark.read.textFile("file:///home/hduser/words")`

7. Divide the line (or lines) into multiple words:

```
words.flatMap(_.split("\\W+"))  (add one more '\' before W)
```

8. Convert `word` to (word,1), that is, output 1 as the value for each occurrence of `word` as a key:

```
scala> val wordsMap = wordsFlatMap.map( w => (w,1))
```

9. Count the occurrence of words:

```
scala> val wordCount = wordsMap.groupByKey(_._1).count
```

10. Print the dataset:

```
scala> wordCount.show
+-----+--------+
|value|count(1)|
+-----+--------+
|  not|       1|
|   be|       2|
|   or|       1|
|   to|       2|
+-----+--------+
```

11. This has no real column names, let's fix it:

```
scala> val wordCountDF = wordCount.toDF("words","count")
```

12. Let's also sort it:

```
scala> val wordCountSorted = wordCountDF.sort(wordCountDF("words"))
```

13. Print the dataset again:

```
scala> wordCountSorted.show
+-----+-----+
|words|count|
+-----+-----+
|   be|    2|
|  not|    1|
|   or|    1|
|   to|    2|
+-----+-----+
```

Loading data from HDFS

HDFS is the second most widely used big data storage system after Amazon S3. One of the reasons for the wide adoption of HDFS is schema on read. What this means is that HDFS does not put any restriction on data when data is being written. Any and all kinds of data are welcome and can be stored in a raw format. This feature makes it the ideal storage for raw unstructured data and semi-structured data.

When it comes to reading data, even unstructured data needs to be given some structure to make sense. Hadoop uses `InputFormat` to determine how to read the data. Spark provides complete support for Hadoop's `InputFormat`, so anything that can be read by Hadoop can be read by Spark as well.

The default `InputFormat` is `TextInputFormat`. `TextInputFormat` takes the byte offset of a line as a key and the content of a line as a value. Spark uses the `spark.read.textFile` method to read using `TextInputFormat`. It ignores the byte offset and creates a dataset of strings.

In this recipe, we will look at how to load data in the Spark shell from HDFS.

How to do it...

Let's do the word count, which counts the number of occurrences of each word. In this recipe, we will load data from HDFS:

1. Create the `words` directory by using the following command:

   ```
   $ mkdir words
   ```

2. Create the `sh.txt` text file and enter "to be or not to be" in it:

   ```
   $ echo "to be or not to be" > words/sh.txt
   ```

3. Upload words:

   ```
   $ hdfs dfs -put words
   ```

4. Start the Spark shell:

   ```
   $ spark-shell
   ```

5. Load the `words` directory as a dataset:

```scala
scala> val words =
spark.read.textFile("hdfs://localhost:9000/user/hduser/words")
```

The `spark.read` method also supports passing an additional option for the number of partitions, such as `spark.read.repartition(10).textFile(...)`. By default, Spark creates one partition for each `InputSplit` class, which roughly corresponds to one block. You can ask for a higher number of partitions. It works really well for compute-intensive jobs, such as in machine learning. As one partition cannot contain more than one block, having fewer partitions than blocks is not allowed.

6. Count the number of lines:

```scala
scala> words.count
```

7. Divide the line (or lines) into multiple words:

```scala
scala> val wordsFlatMap = words.flatMap(_.split("\W+"))
```

8. Convert word to (word,1)—that is, output 1 as a value for each occurrence of `word` as a key:

```scala
scala> val wordsMap = wordsFlatMap.map( w => (w,1))
```

9. Count the occurrences:

```scala
scala> val wordCount =
wordsMap.groupByKey(_._1).count.toDF("word","count")
```

10. Print the dataset:

```scala
scala> wordCount.show
```

Loading data from Amazon S3

If Spark is a MapReduce killer, Amazon S3 is an HDFS killer. S3 is what the ultimate dream of cloud storage can be thought of as. S3 is a foundational service on **Amazon Web Services** (**AWS**), and almost every application running on AWS uses S3 for storage. Not only end-user applications but also other AWS services use S3 extensively; following are a few examples:

- **Amazon Kinesis** uses S3 as target storage
- **Amazon Elastic MapReduce** has one storage mode in S3
- **Amazon Elastic Block Store** (**EBS**) uses S3 to store snapshots
- **Amazon Relation Database Service** (**RDS**) uses S3 to store snapshots
- **Amazon Redshift** uses S3 for data staging
- **Amazon DynamoDB** uses S3 for data staging

Following are some of the salient features of S3:

- 11 9's of durability
- 4 9's of availability
- Typical cost being $30/TB per month while even lower cost options are available

Amazon **Simple Storage Service** (**S3**) provides developers and IT teams with a secure, durable, and scalable storage platform. The biggest advantage of Amazon S3 is that there is no upfront IT investment, and companies can build capacity (just by clicking a button) as they need.

Though Amazon S3 can be used with any compute platform, it integrates really well with Amazon's cloud services, such as Amazon **Elastic Compute Cloud** (**EC2**) and **Amazon Elastic Block Store** (**EBS**). For this reason, companies that use Amazon Web Services are likely to use it as they have significant data already stored on Amazon S3.

This makes a good case for loading data in Spark from Amazon S3, and that is exactly what this recipe is about.

How to do it...

Let's start with the AWS portal:

1. Go to `http://aws.amazon.com`, and log in with your **username** and **password**.
2. Once logged in, navigate to **Storage | S3 | Create Bucket**:

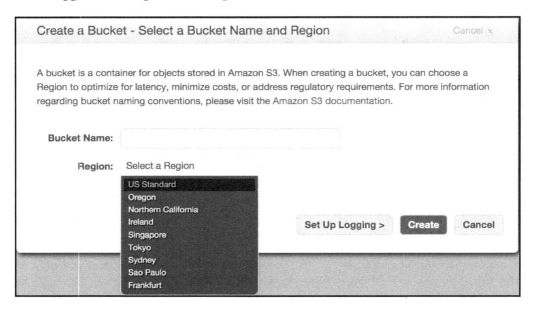

3. Enter the bucket name, for example, `com.infoobjects.wordcount`. Please make sure you enter a unique bucket name (no two S3 buckets can have the same name globally).
4. Select **Region**, click on**Create** and then on the bucket name you created, and you will see the following screen:

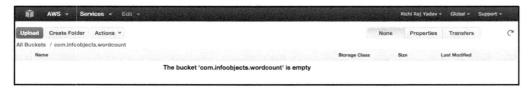

5. Click on **Create Folder** and enter `words` as the folder name.

6. Create the `sh.txt` text file on the local filesystem:

```
$ echo "to be or not to be" > sh.txt
```

7. Navigate to **Words | Upload | Add Files**, and choose `sh.txt` from the dialog box, as shown in the following screenshot:

8. Click on **Start Upload**.

9. Select **sh.txt**, and click on **Properties**, and it will show you details of the file:

10. Set `AWS_ACCESS_KEY` and `AWS_SECRET_ACCESS_KEY` as environment variables.

11. Open the Spark shell, and load the `words` directory from `s3` in the `words` dataset:

```
scala>  val words =
spark.read.textFile("s3a://com.infoobjects.wordcount/words")
```

Now the dataset is loaded, and you can continue doing regular transformations and actions on the dataset.

You can also load data from S3 directly into DataFrames in other formats. For example, here's how you will load JSON data:

```
scala> val ufos =
spark.read.format("json").load("s3a://infoobjects.ufo/ufos")
```

Sometimes there is confusion between `s3://` and `s3a://`. `s3a://` means a regular file sitting in the S3 bucket but readable and writable by the outside world. This filesystem puts a 5 GB limit on the file size. `s3://` means an HDFS file sitting in the S3 bucket. It is a block-based filesystem. The filesystem requires you to dedicate a bucket for this filesystem and is not interoperable with other S3 tools. There is no limit on the file size in this system.

Loading data from Apache Cassandra

Apache Cassandra is a NoSQL database, with a masterless ring cluster structure. While HDFS is a good fit for streaming data access, it does not work well with random access. For example, HDFS will work well when your average file size is 100 MB and you want to read the whole file. If you frequently access the *n*th line in a file or some other part as a record, HDFS would be too slow.

Relational databases have traditionally provided a solution to that, providing low latency, random access, but they do not work well with big data. NoSQL databases, such as Cassandra, fill the gap by providing relational database type access but in a distributed architecture on commodity servers.

In this recipe, we will load data from Cassandra as a Spark DataFrame. To make that happen, Datastax, the company behind Cassandra, has contributed `spark-cassandra-connector`. This package lets you load Cassandra tables as DataFrames, write back to Cassandra, and execute CQL queries.

How to do it...

Perform the following steps to load data from Cassandra:

1. Create a keyspace named `people` in Cassandra using the CQL shell:

```
cqlsh> CREATE KEYSPACE people WITH replication = {'class':
'SimpleStrategy', 'replication_factor': 1 };
```

2. Create a column family (from CQL 3.0 onwards, it can also be called a **table**)
   `person`:

```
cqlsh> use people:
cqlsh> create table person(id int primary key,first_name
varchar,last_name varchar,age int);
```

3. Insert a few records in the column family:

```
cqlsh> insert into person(id, first_name, last_name, age)
values(1,'Barack','Obama',55);
cqlsh> insert into person(id, first_name, last_name, age)
values(2,'Joe','Smith',14);                        cqlsh> insert
into person(id, first_name, last_name, age)
values(3,'Billy','Kid',18);
```

4. Now start the Spark shell with Cassandra connector dependency added:

```
$ spark-shell --packages datastax:spark-cassandra-connector:2.0.0-
M2-s_2.11 --conf spark.cassandra.connection.host=localhost
```

5. Load the `person` table as a DataFrame:

```
scala> val person =
spark.read.format("org.apache.spark.sql.cassandra").options(Map("ke
yspace" ->"people", "table" -> "person")).load
```

6. Print the schema:

```
scala> person.printSchema
root
 |-- name: string (nullable = true)
 |-- age: integer (nullable = true)
```

7. Count the number of records in the DataFrame:

```
scala> person.count
```

8. Print persons DataFrame:

```
scala> person.show
+---+---+----------+---------+
| id|age|first_name|last_name|
+---+---+----------+---------+
|  1| 55|    Barack|    Obama|
|  2| 14|       Joe|    Smith|
|  3| 18|     Billy|      Kid|
+---+---+----------+---------+
```

9. Retrieve the first row:

```
scala> val firstRow = person.first
```

10. Create a `Person` case class:

```
scala> case class Person( first_name:String, last_name:String,
age:Int)
```

11. Create a temporary view out of person DataFrame:

```
scala> person.createOrReplaceTempView("persons")
```

12. Create a DataFrame of teenagers:

```
scala> val teens = spark.sql("select * from persons where age > 12
and age < 20")
```

13. Print the teens DataFrame:

```
scala> teens.show
```

14. Convert it into dataset:

```
scala> val teensDS = teens.as[Person]
```

There are different ways to look at the difference between DataFrame and dataset. Folks who have a hangover from the Hive and Pig days can think of DataFrame being an equivalent of Hive and dataset, Pig.

How it works

Let's discuss the Cassandra architecture.

Here are some of the salient features of the Cassandra architecture:

- Cassandra has a masterless ring architecture
- Data can be written to any node and read from any node
- By default, three replicas are created
- Cassandra comes with built-in datacenter support

CAP Theorem

The CAP Theorem suggests that in distributed architecture, you can pick only two of the following three:

- **Consistency**: Every read gets the most recent copy of the data
- **Availability**: Every request receives a response
- (**Network**) **Partition Tolerance**: The system continues to operate despite network partition

Another way to look at the CAP theorem is: When the network gets partitioned, either consistency or availability can be guaranteed, not both. The following diagram illustrates how the CAP theorem works when the network is partitioned:

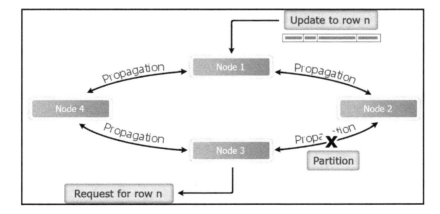

A row is updated in **Node 1** as shown in the preceding figure. Before **Node 3** receives the update propagation, it gets a request for the same row. Now **Node 3** has two choices--either provide the copy of the row it has (which may be stale) or deny the request. In the first case, it is compromising on consistency and in the second case, on availability.

In essence, every distributed database needs to pick its poison. Cassandra has picked consistency to provide high availability.

Cassandra partitions

In Cassandra, the data is stored in the nodes in partitions. A partition is analogous to a row in a relational database. A partition's key is passed to the **murmur3** algorithm to generate a token. The token is used to identify the location of the partition in the cluster. The token is an integer whose value is between 2^{-63} and 2^{63}-1. Hashing distributes data across the cluster so that there is minimum shuffling of partitions when nodes are added or removed. Each node is responsible for partitions belonging to the hash range it has been assigned.

To further ease the pain of redistribution, Cassandra has virtual nodes, or v-nodes, which bundle partitions together. With v-nodes, you do not have to calculate and assign tokens to each node, which helps to rebuild the node faster in case of failure. The following given figure shows rings with and without v-nodes:

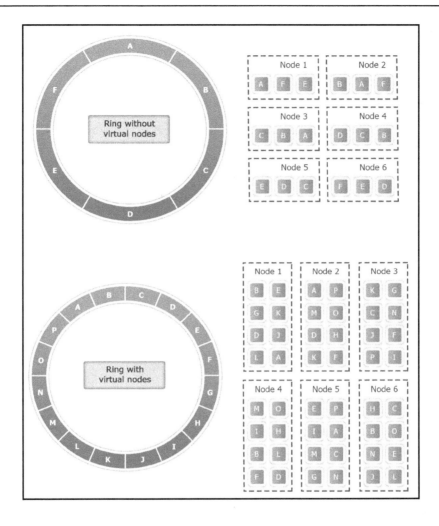

Consistency levels

For read operations, the following three consistency levels are possible:

- **One:** The lowest latency, but dirty reads are possible
- **Quorum:** The middle path
- **All:** The slowest, but data is always good

For write operations, the following three consistency levels are possible:

- **One:** The fastest
- **Quorum:** The middle path
- **All:** The slowest, but data is guaranteed to be written to all the replicas

Cassandra has more fine-grained consistency levels for both read and write, but the aforementioned three are mostly used.

Consistency is a combination of the write and read, and you can have any combination of the two, for example:

- write one, read one
- write one, read quorum
- write quorum, read quorum (recommended)

5
Spark Streaming

Spark Streaming adds the holy grail of big data processing—that is, real-time analytics—to Apache Spark. It enables Spark to ingest live data streams and provides real-time intelligence at a very low latency of a few seconds.

In this chapter, we are going to cover the following recipes:

- WordCount using Structured Streaming
- Diving into Structured Streaming
- Streaming Twitter data
- Streaming using Kafka
- Understanding streaming challenges

Introduction

Streaming is the process of dividing continuously flowing input data into discrete units so that it can be processed easily. Familiar examples in real life are streaming video and audio content (though a user can download the full movie before he/she can watch it, a faster solution is to stream data in small chunks that start playing for the user while the rest of the data is being downloaded in the background).

Real-world examples of streaming, besides multimedia, are the processing of market feeds, weather data, electronic stock trading data, and so on. All these applications produce large volumes of data at very fast rates and require special handling of the data so that you can derive insight from the data in real time.

Streaming has a few basic concepts; it'll be better if we discuss them before we focus on Spark Streaming. The rate at which a streaming application receives data is called **data rate** and is expressed in the form of **kilobytes per second (Kbps)** or **megabytes per second (Mbps)**.

One important use case of streaming is **complex event processing (CEP)**. In CEP, it is important to control the scope of the data being processed. This scope is called **window**, which can be either based on time or size. An example of a time-based window is analyzing data that has come in the last 1 minute. An example of a size-based window can be the average asking price of the last 100 trades of a given stock.

Spark Streaming is Spark's library that provides support to process live data. This stream can come from any source, such as Twitter, Kafka, or Flume.

Spark Streaming has a few fundamental building blocks that you need to understand well before diving into the recipes.

Classic Spark Streaming

Spark Streaming has a context wrapper called `StreamingContext`, which wraps around `SparkContext` and is the entry point to the Spark Streaming functionality. Streaming data, by definition, is continuous and needs to be time-sliced into the process. This slice of time is called a **batch interval**, which is specified when `StreamingContext` is created. There is one-to-one mapping of an RDD and batch; that is, each batch results in one RDD. As you can see in the following image, Spark Streaming takes continuous data, breaks it into batches, and feeds it to Spark:

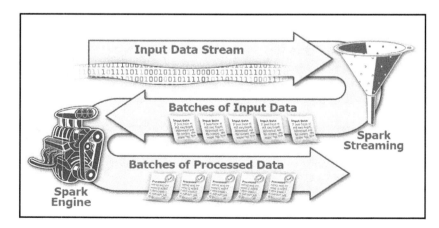

Batch interval is important to optimize your streaming application. Ideally, you want to process data at least as fast as it is getting ingested; otherwise, your application will develop a backlog. Spark Streaming collects data for the duration of a batch interval, say, 2 seconds. The moment this 2-second interval is over, data collected in that interval will be given to Spark for processing, and Streaming will focus on collecting data for the next batch interval. Now, this 2-second batch interval is all Spark has to process data for, as it should be free to receive data from the next batch. If Spark can process the data faster, you can reduce the batch interval to, say, 1 second. If Spark is not able to keep up with this speed, you will have to increase the batch interval.

A continuous stream of RDDs in Spark Streaming needs to be represented in the form of an abstraction through which it can be processed. This abstraction is called **Discretized Stream (DStream)**. Any operation applied to DStream results in an operation on underlying RDDs.

Every input, DStream is associated with a receiver (except for the file stream). A receiver receives data from the input source and stores it in Spark's memory. There are two types of streaming sources:

- Basic sources, such as file and socket connections
- Advanced sources, such as Kafka and Flume

Spark Streaming also provides windowed computations in which you can apply the transformation over a sliding window of data. A sliding window operation is based on two parameters:

- **Window length**: This is the duration of the window. For example, if you want to get analytics of the last 1 minute of data, the window length will be 1 minute.
- **Sliding interval**: This depicts how frequently you want to perform an operation. Say, you want to perform the operation every 10 seconds. This means that every 10 seconds, 1 minute of the window will have 50 seconds of data, which would be common for the last window as well, and 10 seconds of new data.

Structured Streaming

The current API for Spark Streaming is based on DataFrames. This chapter will focus on this new API called Structured Streaming. It is strongly recommended that you use this API, but since it's in beta, some caution needs to be exercised.

WordCount using Structured Streaming

Let's start with a simple example of streaming in which in one terminal, we will type some text and the streaming application will capture it in another window.

How to do it...

1. Start the Spark shell:

   ```
   $ spark-shell
   ```

2. Create a DataFrame to read what's coming on port 8585:

   ```
   scala> val lines =
   spark.readStream.format("socket").option("host","localhost").option
   ("port",8585).load
   ```

3. Cast the lines from DataFrame to Dataset with the String datatype and then flatten it:

   ```
   scala> val words = lines.as[String].flatMap(_.split(" "))
   ```

4. Do the word count:

   ```
   scala> val wordCounts = words.groupBy("value").count()
   ```

5. Start the netcat server in a separate window:

   ```
   $ nc -lk 8585
   ```

6. Come back to the previous terminal and print the complete set of counts to the console every time it is updated:

   ```
   scala> val query =
   wordCounts.writeStream.outputMode("complete").format("console").sta
   rt()
   ```

7. Now go back to the terminal where you started netcat and enter different lines, such as to be or not to be:

   ```
   to be or not to be
   ```

8. See the output live on the other screen:

```
------------------------------------------
Batch: 0
------------------------------------------
+-----+-----+
|value|count|
+-----+-----+
|  not|    1|
|   be|    2|
|   hi|    1|
|   or|    1|
|   to|    2|
+-----+-----+
```

Taking a closer look at Structured Streaming

Structured Streaming has been introduced in various places in this chapter, but let's use this recipe to discuss some more details. Structured Streaming is essentially a stream-processing engine built on top of the Spark SQL engine.

An alternative way to look at streaming data is to think of it as an infinite/unbounded table that gets continuously appended as new data arrives.

The four fundamental concepts in Structured Streaming are:

- **Input table**: To input the table
- **Trigger**: How often the table gets updated
- **Result table**: The final table after every trigger update
- **Output table**: What part of the result to write to storage after every trigger

A query may be interested in only newly appended data (since the last query), all of the data that has been updated (including appended obviously), or the whole table; this leads to the three output modes in Structured Streaming, as follows:

- Append
- Update
- Complete

The DataFrame/Dataset API that is used for bounded tables works here in exactly the same way and that means that continuously streaming data can be queried using regular SQL or DSL commands. Let's do an example of how it differs from the static DataFrame.

How to do it...

1. Start the Spark shell:

   ```
   $ spark-shell
   ```

2. Read diabetes data from `s3` as DataFrame (static):

   ```scala
   scala> val sdf
   = spark.read.format("libsvm").load("s3a://sparkcookbook/patientdata
   ")
   ```

3. Extract schema from `sdf` DataFrame:

   ```scala
   scala> val schema = sdf.schema
   ```

4. Read diabetes data as Streaming DataFrame:

   ```scala
   scala> val st_df
   = spark.readStream.schema(schema).format("libsvm").load("s3a://spar
   kcookbook/patientdata")
   ```

5. Choose only the data that is positive, that is, has diabetes:

   ```scala
   scala> val result = st_df.where($"label" === 1.0)
   ```

6. Write this data to `hdfs`:

   ```scala
   scala>
   result.writeStream.option("checkpointLocation", "cp").format("parque
   t").start("tested-positive")
   ```

There's more...

One addition that Structured Streaming has done under the hood is adding the incremental plan execution. To understand it better, let's revisit a diagram from the *Understanding the Catalyst optimizer* recipe from `Chapter 3`, *Spark SQL*:

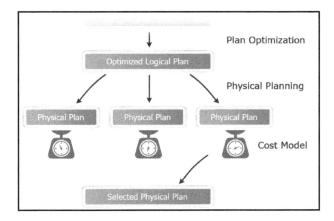

So the planner is aware that when streaming the logical plan, it should be converted into incremental physical execution plans.

Streaming Twitter data

Twitter is a famous microblogging platform. It produces a massive amount of data with around 500 million tweets sent each day. Twitter allows its data to be accessed by APIs, and that makes it the poster child of testing any big data streaming application.

In this recipe, we will see how we can live stream data in Spark using Twitter-streaming libraries. Twitter is just one source of providing streaming data to Spark and has no special status. Therefore, there are no built-in libraries for Twitter. Spark does provide some APIs to facilitate the integration with Twitter libraries, though.

An example use of a live Twitter data feed can be to find trending tweets in the last 5 minutes.

How to do it...

1. Create a Twitter account if you do not already have one.
2. Go to `http://apps.twitter.com`.
3. Click on **Create New App**.
4. Fill out the **Name**, **Description**, **Website**, and **Callback URL** fields and then click on **Create your Twitter Application**. You will receive a screen like this:

5. You will reach the **Application Management** screen.
6. Navigate to **Keys and Access Tokens** | **Create my access Token**:

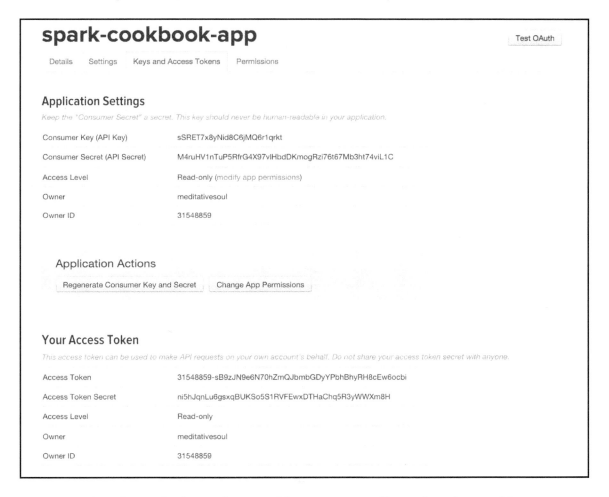

7. Note down the four values on this screen; we will use them in step 14:

- Consumer key (the API Key)
- Consumer secret (the API Secret)
- Access token
- Access token secret

8. Fill in the values on this screen in some time, but, for now, let's download the third-party libraries needed from Maven central:

```
$ wget
http://central.maven.org/maven2/org/apache/spark/spark-streaming-tw
itter_2.10/1.2.0/spark-streaming-twitter_2.10-1.2.0.jar
$ wget
http://central.maven.org/maven2/org/twitter4j/twitter4j-stream/4.0.
2/twitter4j-stream-4.0.2.jar
$ wget
http://central.maven.org/maven2/org/twitter4j/twitter4j-core/4.0.2/
twitter4j-core-4.0.2.jar
```

9. Open the Spark shell, supplying the preceding three JARs as dependencies:

```
$ spark-shell --packages org.twitter4j:twitter4j-
core:4.0.5,org.twitter4j:twitter4j-stream:4.0.5 --jars dstream-
twitter_2.11-0.1.0.jar
```

10. Perform imports that are Twitter-specific:

```
scala> import org.apache.spark.streaming.twitter._
scala> import twitter4j.auth._
scala> import twitter4j.conf._
```

11. Stream specific imports:

```
scala> import org.apache.spark.streaming.{Seconds,
StreamingContext}
```

12. Do necessary imports:

```
scala>import org.apache.spark._
scala> import org.apache.spark.streaming._
scala> import org.apache.spark.streaming.StreamingContext._
```

13. Create `StreamingContext` with a 10-second batch interval:

```
scala> val ssc = new StreamingContext(spark.sparkContext,
Seconds(10))
```

14. Create `StreamingContext` with a 2-second batch interval:

```
scala> val cb = new ConfigurationBuilder
scala>cb.setDebugEnabled(true)
  .setOAuthConsumerKey("FKNryYEKeCrKzGV7zuZW4EKeN")
  .setOAuthConsumerSecret("x6Y0zcTBOwVxpvekSCnGzbi3NYN
```

```
rM5b8ZMZRIPI1XRC3pDyOs1")
   .setOAuthAccessToken("31548859-DHbESdk6YoghCLcfhMF8
8QEFDvEjxbM6Q90eoZTG1")
   .setOAuthAccessTokenSecret("wjcWPvtejZSbp9cgLejUdd6W1
MJqFzm51ByUFZ11NYgrV")
val auth = new OAuthAuthorization(cb.build)
```

These are sample values; you put your own values.

15. Create Twitter's DStream:

    ```
    scala> val tweets = TwitterUtils.createStream(ssc,auth)
    ```

16. Filter out English tweets:

    ```
    scala> val englishTweets = tweets.filter(_.getLang()=="en")
    ```

17. Get the text out of the tweets:

    ```
    scala> val status = englishTweets.map(status => status.getText)
    ```

18. Set the checkpoint directory:

    ```
    scala>
    ssc.checkpoint("hdfs://localhost:9000/user/hduser/checkpoint")
    ```

19. Start `StreamingContext`:

    ```
    scala> ssc.start
    scala> ssc.awaitTermination
    ```

20. You can put all these commands together using `:paste`:

    ```
    scala> :paste
    import org.apache.spark.streaming.twitter._
    import twitter4j.auth._
    import twitter4j.conf._
    import org.apache.spark.streaming.{Seconds, StreamingContext}
    import org.apache.spark._
    import org.apache.spark.streaming._
    import org.apache.spark.streaming.StreamingContext._
    val ssc = new StreamingContext(sc, Seconds(10))
    val cb = new ConfigurationBuilder
    cb.setDebugEnabled(true).setOAuthConsumerKey("FKNryYEKe
    ```

```
CrKzGV7zuZW4EKeN")
  .setOAuthConsumerSecret("x6Y0zcTBOwVxpvekSCnGzbi3NYNr
M5b8ZMZRIPI1XRC3pDyOs1")
  .setOAuthAccessToken("31548859-DHbESdk6YoghCLcfhMF88Q
EFDvEjxbM6Q90eoZTGl")
  .setOAuthAccessTokenSecret("wjcWPvtejZSbp9cgLejUdd6W1
MJqFzm51ByUFZl1NYgrV")
val auth = new OAuthAuthorization(cb.build)
val tweets = TwitterUtils.createStream(ssc,Some(auth))
val englishTweets = tweets.filter(_.getLang()=="en")
val status = englishTweets.map(status => status.getText)
status.print
ssc.checkpoint("hdfs://localhost:9000/checkpoint")
ssc.start
ssc.awaitTermination
```

Streaming using Kafka

Kafka is a distributed, partitioned, and replicated commit log service. In simple words, it is a distributed messaging server. Kafka maintains the message feed in categories called **topics**. An example of a topic can be the ticker symbol of a company you would like to get news about, for example, **CSCO** for **Cisco**.

Processes that produce messages are called **producers** and those that consume messages are called **consumers**. In traditional messaging, the messaging service has one central messaging server, also called the **broker**. Since Kafka is a distributed messaging service, it has a cluster of brokers, which functionally acts as one Kafka broker, as shown here:

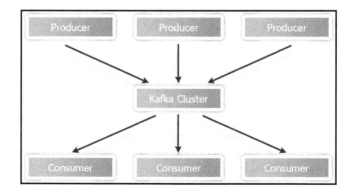

For each topic, Kafka maintains the partitioned log. This partitioned log consists of one or more partitions spread across the cluster, as shown in the following figure:

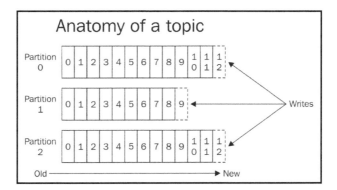

Kafka borrows a lot of concepts from Hadoop and other big data frameworks. The concept of partition is very similar to the concept of `InputSplit` in Hadoop. In the simplest form, while using `TextInputFormat`, an `InputSplit` is the same as a block. A block is read in the form of a key-value pair in `TextInputFormat`, where the key is the byte offset of a line and the value is the content of the line itself. In a similar way, in a Kafka partition, records are stored and retrieved in the form of key-value pairs, where the key is a sequential ID number called the **offset** and the value is the actual message.

In Kafka, message retention does not depend on the consumption of a consumer. Messages are retained for a configurable period of time. Each consumer is free to read messages in any order they like. All they need to do is retain an offset. Another analogy can be reading a book in which the page number is analogous to the offset, while the page content is analogous to the message. The reader is free to read whichever way he/she wants as long as they remember the bookmark (the current offset).

To provide functionality similar to pub/sub and PTP (queues) in traditional messaging systems, Kafka has the concept of consumer groups. A consumer group is a group of consumers, which the Kafka cluster treats as a single unit. In a consumer group, only one consumer needs to receive a message. If the **C1** consumer, in the following diagram, receives the first message for the topic **T1**, all the following messages on that topic will also be delivered to this consumer. Using this strategy, Kafka guarantees the order of message delivery for a given topic.

In extreme cases, when all consumers are in one consumer group, the Kafka cluster acts like PTP/queue. In another extreme case, if every consumer belongs to a different group, it acts like pub/sub. In practice, each consumer group has a limited number of consumers:

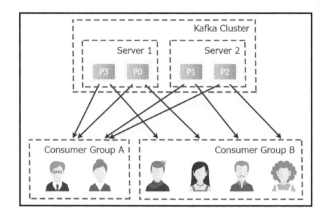

This recipe will show you how to perform a word count using the data coming from Kafka.

Getting ready

This recipe assumes you already have Kafka up and running. Let us create a topic `oscars` in Kafka for this recipe:

```
$ kafka-topics.sh --create --zookeeper localhost:2181 --
replication-factor 1 --partitions 1 --topic oscars
```

How to do it...

1. Start the Spark shell with the Kafka integration package:

```
$ spark-shell --packages org.apache.spark:spark-sql-
kafka-0-10_2.11:2.1.1
```

2. Create a stream to listen to messages for the `oscars` topic:

```
scala> val data =
spark.readStream.format("kafka").option("kafka.bootstrap.servers","
localhost:9092").option("subscribe","oscars").load()
```

3. To find out if it is really a streaming DataFrame or not:

```scala
scala> data.isStreaming
```

4. Get the schema of data DataFrame:

```scala
scala> data.printSchema
```

5. Create a stream to listen to messages for the `oscars` topic:

```scala
scala> val data =
spark.readStream.format("kafka").option("kafka.bootstrap.servers","
localhost:9092").option("subscribe","oscars").load()
```

6. Cast the stream to `String` datatype:

```scala
scala> val kvstream = data.selectExpr("CAST(key AS STRING)",
"CAST(value AS STRING)")
```

7. Write the stream to console based receiver and keep it running until terminated:

```scala
scala> val feed = kvstream.writeStream.format("console").start
scala> feed.awaitTermination
```

8. Publish a message on the `oscars` topic in Kafka in another window:

```
$ kafka-console-producer.sh --broker-list localhost:9092 --topic
oscars
```

9. Now, publish messages on Kafka by pressing **Enter** at *step 8* and after every message.

10. Now as you publish messages on Kafka, you will see them in the Spark shell.

Understanding streaming challenges

There are certain challenges every streaming application faces. In this recipe, we will develop some understanding of these challenges.

Late arriving/out-of-order data

If there is leader selection in streaming challenges, it would go to the late data. This is such a streaming-specific issue that folks not very familiar with streaming find it surprising that this issue is so prevalent.

There are two notions of time in streaming:

- **Event time**: This is the time when an event actually happened, for example, measuring the temperature on a drive to an industrial site. Almost always, this event will contain this time as part of the record.
- **Processing time**: This is measured by the program that processed the event, for example, if the time series IoT event is processed in the cloud, then the processing time is the time this event reached the component (like Kinesis), which is doing the processing.

In stream-processing applications, this time lag between the event time and processing time varies, and this leads to late or out-of-order data. There are various reasons for this delay, for example:

- Network latencies
- Variance in data load
- Batching of events

In Spark Streaming based on `DStream`, it is not easy to incorporate event time.

Maintaining the state in between batches

In microbatch-based streaming systems, such as Spark, sometimes the state needs to be maintained and/or updated in between batches. In the current Spark implementation, there are various ways to do this, for example, windowing and `updateStateByKey`. In all these ways, essentially, a join operation is done on batches to maintain the state. This can get very expensive if the window length is long. Another option is to maintain the state in a database. There are in-memory databases, such as **MemSQL**, but they come with the cost of maintaining the overhead of another database system.

Structured Streaming has rewritten state management to maintain this running intermediate state in the memory, backed by **write ahead logs** (**WAL**) in the file system for fault-tolerance.

Message delivery reliability

There are a few message delivery semantics on which message delivery guarantees (or lack of them) are based:

- **At most one delivery**: This means the message will be delivered zero or one times. It means the message may be lost. It's the cheapest way and is also known as **fire and forget**.
- **At least one delivery**: This means in multiple delivery attempts, there may be a chance that the message may be duplicated, but it will not be lost for sure.
- **Exactly one delivery**: This means that the message is only delivered once. It's neither getting lost or duplicated.

Structured Streaming provides an end-to-end and exactly one message delivery guarantee based on the following features:

- Offset tracking in WAL
- State management (using the in-memory state and WAL)
- Fault-tolerant sources and sinks (using WAL)

Streaming is not an island

Streaming apps are never standalone applications, but part of a larger ecosystem. First, a streaming application may ingest data from complex data sources. Data may come from relational and non-relational sources. Data can be of various formats, such as `.json` and `.avro`. Data can be at various levels of normalization. To add to it, every real data source has tons of dirty data; this can lead to a massive cycle of data cleaning and data preparation.

Streaming applications may interface with interactive analytics apps or machine-learning apps. It means there are throughput and scalability challenges that need to be resolved differently in each case. There are a few tips that can help in this optimization:

- **Data temperature awareness**: All of the data is not created in the same way, and all of the data does not need to be treated the same way. There is the temperature of the data (how recent the data is) and the importance of data, which are correlated. One example can be online machine learning for fraud detection where the latency **service level agreement** (**SLA**) is in milliseconds. You may also want to update your ML model in real time, based on the data you are getting.
- **Avoiding persisting on disk**: Persisting/checkpointing data on the disk is an expensive operation and something that killed MapReduce (besides other factors). Maximize the use of memory.

6
Getting Started with Machine Learning

This chapter is divided into the following recipes:

- Creating vectors
- Calculating correlation
- Understanding feature engineering
- Understanding Spark ML
- Understanding hyperparameter tuning

Introduction

The following is Wikipedia's definition of machine learning:

> *"Machine learning is a scientific discipline that explores the construction and study of algorithms that can learn from data."*

Essentially, machine learning is the process of using past data to make predictions about the future. Machine learning heavily depends upon statistical analysis and methodology.

In statistics, there are four types of measurement scales:

Scale type	Description
Nominal scale	• =, ≠ • Identifies categories • Can't be numeric • Example: male, female
Ordinal scale	• =, ≠, <, > • Nominal scale + • Ranks from least important to most important • Example: corporate hierarchy
Interval scale	• =, ≠, <, >, +, - • Ordinal scale + distance between observations • Numbers assigned to observations indicate order • Difference between any consecutive values is same as others • 60° temperature is not doubly hot than 30°
Ratio scale	• =, ≠, <, >, +, ×, ÷ • Interval scale +ratios of observations • \$20 is twice as costly as \$10

Another distinction that can be made among the data is continuous versus discrete data. Continuous data can take any value, for example, house price. Most data belonging to the interval and ratio scale is continuous.

Discrete variables can take on only particular values, and there are clear boundaries between the values. For example, a house can have two or three rooms but not 2.75 rooms. Data belonging to the nominal and ordinal scale is always discrete.

MLlib is Spark's library for machine learning. Like other libraries, MLlib's algorithms have slowly been ported to make them DataFrame-based as opposed to RDD-based. These ported algorithms are sometimes called **ML**; technically, however, it is still MLlib. In this chapter, we will focus on the fundamentals of machine learning.

Creating vectors

Before understanding vectors, let's focus on what a point is. A point is just a set of numbers. This set of numbers or coordinates defines the point's position in space. The number of coordinates determines the dimensions of the space.

We can visualize space with up to three dimensions. A space with more than three dimensions is called **hyperspace**. Let's put this spatial metaphor to use.

Getting ready

Let's start with a house. A house may have the following dimensions:

- Area
- Lot size
- Number of rooms

We are working in three-dimensional space here. Thus, the interpretation of point (4500, 41000, 4) would be 4500 sq. ft area, 41k sq. ft lot size, and four rooms.

Points and vectors are the same thing. Dimensions in vectors are called **features**. In another way, we can define a feature as an individual measurable property of a phenomenon being observed.

Spark has local vectors and matrices and also distributed matrices. A distributed matrix is backed by one or more RDDs. A local vector has numeric indices and double values and is stored on a single machine.

There are two types of local vectors in MLlib: **dense** and **sparse**. A dense vector is backed by an array of its values, while a sparse vector is backed by two parallel arrays, one for indices and another for values.

So, house data (4500, 41000, 4) will be represented as [4500, 41000, 4] using dense vector and as (3, [0, 1, 2], [4500.0, 41000.0, 4.0]) using sparse vector format.

Whether to make a vector sparse or dense depends upon how many null values or 0s it has. Let's take the case of a vector with 10,000 values, 9,000 of them being 0. If we use the dense vector format, it would be a simple structure, but 90 per cent of the space will be wasted. The sparse vector format would work out better here as it would only keep indices, which are non-zero.

Sparse data is very common, and Spark now natively supports the libsvm format for it, which stores one feature vector per line.

How to do it...

1. Start the Spark shell:

   ```
   $ spark-shell
   ```

2. Import the MLlib vector explicitly (not to be confused with other vector classes in collections):

   ```
   scala> import org.apache.spark.ml.linalg.{Vector, Vectors}
   ```

3. Create a dense vector:

   ```
   scala> val denseHouse = Vectors.dense(4500d,41000d,4d)
   ```

4. Create a sparse vector:

   ```
   scala> val sparseHouse =
   Vectors.sparse(3,Array(0,1,2),Array(4500d,41000d,4d))
   ```

5. Create a vector of all zeroes:

   ```
   scala> val zeroes = Vectors.zeros(3)
   ```

How it works...

The following is the method signature of `vectors.dense`:

```
def dense(values: Array[Double]): Vector
```

Here, values represent a double array of elements in the vector.

The following is the method signature of `Vectors.sparse`:

```
def sparse(size: Int, indices: Array[Int], values: Array[Double]): Vector
```

Here, `size` represents the size of the vector, `indices` is an array of indices, and `values` is an array of values as doubles. Do make sure you specify `double` as a datatype or use decimal in at least one value; otherwise, it will throw an exception for the dataset, which has only integer.

Calculating correlation

Correlation is a statistical relationship between two variables such that when one variable changes, it leads to a change in the other variable. Correlation analysis measures the extent to which the two variables are correlated.

We see correlation in our daily life. The height of a person is correlated with the weight of a person, the load carrying capacity of a truck is correlated with the number of wheels it has, and so on.

If an increase in one variable leads to an increase in another, it is called a **positive correlation**. If an increase in one variable leads to a decrease in the other, it is a **negative correlation**.

Spark supports two correlation algorithms: **Pearson** and **Spearman**. The Pearson algorithm works with two continuous variables, such as a person's height and weight or house size and house price. Spearman deals with one continuous and one categorical variable, for example, zip code and house price.

Getting ready

Let's use some real data so that we can calculate correlation more meaningfully. The following were the sizes and prices of houses in the City of Saratoga, California, in early 2014:

House size (sq ft)	Price
2100	$1,620,000
2300	$1,690,000
2046	$1,400,000
4314	$2,000,000
1244	$1,060,000
4608	$3,830,000
2173	$1,230,000
2750	$2,400,000
4010	$3,380,000
1959	$1,480,000

How to do it...

1. Start the Spark shell:

    ```
    $ spark-shell
    ```

2. Create a DataFrame of house price and size:

    ```scala
    scala>  val houses = spark.createDataFrame(Seq(
    (1620000d,2100),
    (1690000d,2300),
    (1400000d,2046),
    (2000000d,4314),
    (1060000d,1244),
    (3830000d,4608),
    (1230000d,2173),
    (2400000d,2750),
    (3380000d,4010),
    (1480000d,1959)
    )).toDF("price","size")
    ```

3. Compute the correlation:

    ```scala
    scala> houses.stat.corr("price","size")
    correlation: Double = 0.8577177736252574
    ```

     Since we do not have a specific algorithm here, it is, by default, Pearson. The `corr` method is overloaded to take the algorithm name as the third parameter. `0.85` means a very strong positive correlation.

4. Compute the correlation with Pearson passed explicitly as a parameter:

    ```scala
    scala> houses.stat.corr("price","size","pearson")
                correlation: Double = 0.8577177736252574
    ```

Understanding feature engineering

When working on a data pipeline, there are two activities that take up most of the time: data cleaning/data preparation and feature extraction. We already covered data cleaning in the previous chapters. In this recipe, we are going to discuss different aspects of feature engineering.

Feature selection

When it comes to feature selection, there are two primary aspects:

- Quality of features
- Number of features

Quality of features

Every feature is created different from others. Consider the house pricing problem again. Let's look at some of the features of a house:

- House size
- Lot size
- Number of rooms
- Number of bathrooms
- Type of parking garage (carport versus covered)
- School district
- Number of dogs barking in the house
- Number of birds chirping in backyard trees

The last two features may look ridiculous to you, and you might wonder what that has got to do with the house price, and you are right. At the same time, if these features are given to the machine learning algorithm, it may come up with a non-zero correlation to your surprise. This is where domain knowledge comes into the picture. It could be a data scientist wearing a domain expert hat or a domain expert wearing a data scientist hat, who would most likely do this job.

Number of features

Having too many and irrelevant features adds unnecessary noise. They also make machine learning models difficult and more expensive to train.

At the same time, what if we take another extreme. What if we use only house size as a feature to make predictions. As we saw in the previous recipe, house size is the most influential feature, but it would not bring the quality of prediction to an acceptable level. We need a reasonable number of features to make accurate predictions.

Feature scaling

Features can be on four scales as we covered in the introduction of this chapter. Models do not care about nominal features but are very sensitive to the scale of ratio or numerical features. In the house example, the house size and lot size are on a different scale, and that may make the model think that the lot size is more important than the house size, though the truth is quite the opposite. In a lot of real-life modeling scenarios, scale difference can be in hundreds, if not in thousands.

There are different ways of doing feature scaling, such as the following:

- Dividing a feature value with a maximum value, which will put every feature in the range
- Dividing a feature value with the range, that is, maximum value-minimum value
- Subtracting a feature value by its mean and then dividing by the range
- Subtracting a feature value by its mean and then dividing by the standard deviation

Feature extraction

We can only select features if we have them in the first place. This is where the role of feature extraction comes.

TF-IDF

Term frequency inverse document frequency (TF-IDF), is a numerical statistic that is intended to reflect how important a word is to a document in a collection or corpus. Let's denote a term by t, document by d, and corpus by D.

Term frequency

Let us say we mean a page by a document (could be a chapter as well) and the whole book by a corpus. In a document, we can simply measure how many times a term has occurred. The more times a term has occurred, the more important it is in the document. But is that really the case? We will end up with articles (a/an/the) being on top of the list every time. Let's define term frequency as $TF(t, d)$.

Inverse document frequency

What if we also measure how many times a term has occurred across the corpus. If a term has occurred across the corpus with the same frequency, then it is not so important to the specific document. Let's say term frequency across the corpus is $DF(t, D)$. Average frequency per document will be as follows:

$$DF(t, D)/|D|$$

Here, $|D|$ is the number of documents. Since the importance of a term is inversely proportional to $DF(t, D)$, let's inverse it and take a log:

$$log\ |D|/DF(t, D)$$

Now it looks good, except that when the number of documents is 0, the log becomes undefined. So let's add 1 to both the numerator and the denominator to avoid the boundary condition:

$$(log\ |D| + 1\ )/ (DF(t, D) + 1)$$

This is called **inverse document frequency**:

$$IDF(t, D) = (log\ |D| + 1\ )/ (DF(t, D) + 1)$$

Multiplying TF and IDF results in TF-IDF:

$$TFIDF(t,d,D) = TF(t,d) \times IDF(t,D)$$

How to do it...

1. Load Spark shell or Databricks Cloud:

    ```
    $ spark-shell
    ```

2. Do the necessary imports:

    ```scala
    scala> import org.apache.spark.ml.feature._
    ```

3. Load the Charles Dickens novel *Hard Times*:

```scala
scala> val sentenceData =
spark.read.option("delimiter","\n").csv
("s3a://sparkcookbook/hardtimes").toDF("sentence")
```

4. Create a transformer to tokenize sentences:

```scala
scala> val tokenizer = new
Tokenizer().setInputCol("sentence").setOutputCol("words")
```

5. Tokenize sentences:

```scala
scala> val wordsData = tokenizer.transform(sentenceData)
```

6. Create a hashing transformer:

```scala
scala> val hashingTF = new HashingTF()
.setInputCol("words").setOutputCol("rawFeatures").setNumFeatures(20)
```

7. Map the sequence of terms to term frequencies:

```scala
scala> val featurizedData = hashingTF.transform(wordsData)
```

8. Create an IDF estimator:

```scala
scala> val idf = new
IDF().setInputCol("rawFeatures").setOutputCol("features")
```

9. Train the IDF model:

```scala
scala> val idfModel = idf.fit(featurizedData)
```

10. Rescale TF based on the IDF model:

```scala
scala> val rescaledData = idfModel.transform(featurizedData)
```

11. Print the results:

```scala
scala> rescaledData.show()
```

Understanding Spark ML

Spark ML is a nickname for the DataFrame-based MLLib API. Spark ML is the primary library now, and the RDD-based API has been moved to maintenance mode.

Getting ready

Let's first understand some of the basic concepts in Spark ML. Before that, let's quickly go over how the learning process works. Following are the steps:

1. A machine learning algorithm is provided a training dataset along with the right hyperparameters.
2. The result of training is a model. The following figure illustrates the model building by applying machine learning algorithm on training data with hyperparameters:

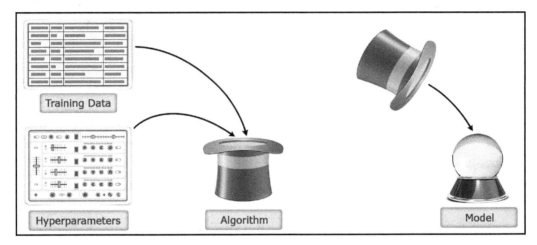

3. The model is then used to make predictions on test data as shown here:

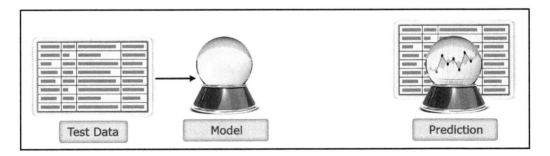

In Spark ML, an estimator is provided as a DataFrame (via the `fit` method), and the output after training is a Transformer:

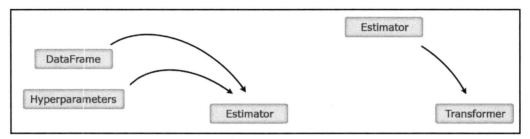

Now, the Transformer takes one DataFrame as input and outputs another transformed (via the `transform` method) DataFrame. For example, it can take a DataFrame with the test data and enrich this DataFrame with an additional column for predictions and then output it as shown here:

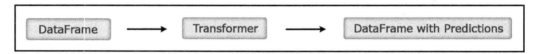

Transformers are not just limited to doing predictions on models but can also be used to do feature transformation. An easy way to understand feature transformation is to compare it to the map function in RDDs.

A machine learning pipeline is defined as a sequence of stages; each stage can be either an estimator or a Transformer.

The example we are going to use in this recipe is whether or not someone is a basketball player. For this, we are going to have a pipeline of one estimator and one Transformer.

The estimator gets the training data to train the algorithms, and then the Transformer makes predictions.

Please note that both `Transformer.transform()` and `Estimator.fit()` are stateless.

For now, assume `LogisticRegression` to be the machine learning algorithm we are using. We will explain the details about `LogisticRegression` along with other algorithms in the subsequent chapters.

How to do it...

1. Start the Spark shell:

   ```
   $ spark-shell
   ```

2. Do the imports:

   ```
   scala> import org.apache.spark.ml.classification.LogisticRegression
   scala> import org.apache.spark.ml.linalg.{Vector, Vectors}
   ```

3. Create a tuple for Lebron, who is a basketball player, is 80 inches tall, and weighs 250 lbs:

   ```
   scala> val lebron = (1.0,Vectors.dense(80.0,250.0))
   ```

4. Create a tuple for Tim, who is not a basketball player, is 70 inches tall, and weighs 150 lbs:

   ```
   scala> val tim = (0.0,Vectors.dense(70.0,150.0))
   ```

5. Create a tuple for Brittany, who is a basketball player, is 80 inches tall, and weighs 207 lbs:

   ```
   scala> val brittany = (1.0,Vectors.dense(80.0,207.0))
   ```

6. Create a tuple for Stacey, who is not a basketball player, is 65 inches tall, and weighs 120 lbs:

   ```
   scala> val stacey = (0.0,Vectors.dense(65.0,120.0))
   ```

8. Create a training DataFrame:

   ```
   scala> val training = spark.createDataFrame(Seq
   (lebron,tim,brittany,stacey)).toDF("label","features")
   ```

9. Create a `LogisticRegression` estimator:

   ```
   scala> val estimator = new LogisticRegression
   ```

10. Create a transformer by fitting the estimator with the training DataFrame:

    ```
    scala> val transformer = estimator.fit(training)
    ```

11. Now, let's create a test data—John is 90 inches tall, weighs 270 lbs, and is a basketball player:

```scala
scala> val john = Vectors.dense(90.0,270.0)
```

12. Create more test data—Tom is 62 inches tall, weighs 150 lbs, and is not a basketball player:

```scala
scala> val tom = Vectors.dense(62.0,120.0)
```

13. Create a test data DataFrame:

```scala
scala> val test = spark.createDataFrame(Seq(
  (1.0, john),
  (0.0, tom)
)).toDF("label", "features")
```

14. Do the prediction using the transformer:

```scala
scala> val results = transformer.transform(test)
```

15. Print the schema of the results DataFrame:

```scala
scala> results.printSchema
```

```
root
|-- label: double (nullable = false)
|-- features: vector (nullable = true)
|-- rawPrediction: vector (nullable = true)
|-- probability: vector (nullable = true)
|-- prediction: double (nullable = true)
```

As you can see, besides prediction, the transformer has also added `rawPrediction` and a probability column.

16. Print the DataFrame results:

```scala
scala> results.show
```

```
+-----+------------+--------------------+--------------------+----------+
|label|    features|       rawPrediction|         probability|prediction|
+-----+------------+--------------------+--------------------+----------+
|  1.0|[90.0,270.0]|[-61.884758625897...|[1.32981373684616...|       1.0|
|  0.0|[62.0,120.0]|[31.4607691062275...|[0.99999999999997...|       0.0|
+-----+------------+--------------------+--------------------+----------+
```

17. Let's select only `features` and `prediction`:

```
scala> val predictions = results.select
("features","prediction").show

+------------+----------+
| features|prediction|
+------------+----------+
|[90.0,270.0]| 1.0|
|[62.0,120.0]| 0.0|
+------------+----------+
```

Understanding hyperparameter tuning

Every ML algorithm (let's start calling it estimator from now on) needs some hyperparameters to be set before it can be trained. These hyperparameters have traditionally been set by hand. Some examples of hyperparameters are step size, number of steps (learning rate), regularization parameters, and so on.

Typically, hyperparameter tuning is a detour in model selection as you already need to know the best value of hyperparameters for training the model. At the same time, to find the right hyperparameters, you need to be able to look ahead at the accuracy. This is where evaluators come into the picture.

In this recipe, we are going to consider an example of linear regression. The focus here is on hyperparameter tuning, so details about linear regression are skipped and covered in depth in the next chapter.

How to do it...

1. Start Spark shell:

```
$ spark-shell
```

2. Do the necessary imports:

```
scala> import org.apache.spark.ml.regression.LinearRegression
scala> import org.apache.spark.ml.evaluation.RegressionEvaluator
scala> import org.apache.spark.ml.tuning.{ParamGridBuilder,
TrainValidationSplit}
```

3. Load data as DataFrame:

```scala
scala> val data =
spark.read.format("libsvm").load
("s3a://sparkcookbook/housingdata/realestate.libsvm")
```

4. Split data into training and test sets:

```scala
scala> val Array(training, test) = data.randomSplit
(Array(0.7, 0.3))
```

5. Instantiate linear regression:

```scala
scala> val lr = new LinearRegression().setMaxIter(10)
```

6. Create a parameter grid:

```scala
scala> val paramGrid = new ParamGridBuilder()
 .addGrid(lr.regParam, Array(0.1,0.01))
 .addGrid(lr.fitIntercept)
 .addGrid(lr.elasticNetParam, Array(0.0, 0.5, 1.0))
 .build()
```

7. Create a training validation split:

```scala
scala> val trainValidationSplit = new TrainValidationSplit()
 .setEstimator(lr)
 .setEvaluator(new RegressionEvaluator)
 .setEstimatorParamMaps(paramGrid)
 .setTrainRatio(0.8)
```

8. Train the model:

```scala
scala> val model = trainValidationSplit.fit(training)
```

9. Do the predictions on the test dataset:

```scala
scala> val predictions = model.transform(test)
```

10. Evaluate the predictions:

```scala
scala> val evaluator = new RegressionEvaluator()
scala> evaluator.evaluate(predictions)
```

7
Supervised Learning with MLib — Regression

This chapter is divided into the following recipes:

- Using linear regression
- Understanding the cost function
- Doing linear regression with lasso
- Doing ridge regression

Introduction

The following is Wikipedia's definition of supervised learning:

> *"Supervised learning is the machine learning task of inferring a function from labeled training data."*

There are two types of supervised learning algorithms:

- **Regression**: This predicts a continuous valued output, such as a house price.
- **Classification**: This predicts a discreet valued output (0 or 1) called **label**, such as whether an e-mail is a spam or not. Classification is not limited to two values (binomial); it can have multiple values (multinomial), such as marking an e-mail important, unimportant, urgent, and so on (0, 1, 2...).

We are going to cover regression in this chapter and classification in the next.

We will use the recently sold house data of the City of Saratoga, CA, as an example to illustrate the steps of supervised learning in the case of regression:

1. Get the labeled data:

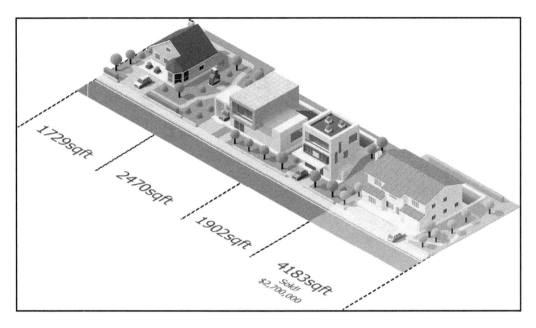

- How labeled data is gathered differs in every use case. For example, to convert paper documents into a digital format, documents can be given to Amazon Mechanical Turk to label them.
- The size of the labeled data needs to be sufficiently larger than the number of features in the vector. If the size is small compared to the number of features, it can result in overfitting.

2. Split the labeled data into two parts:

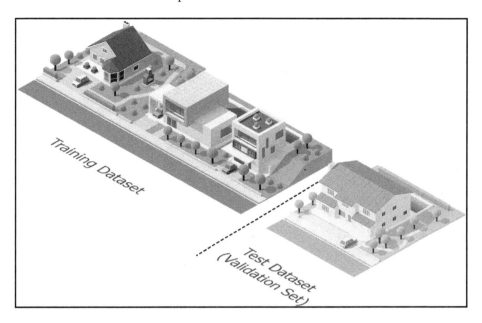

- Randomly split the data based on a certain ratio, for example, 70:30.
- This split needs to be done randomly every time to avoid bias.
- The first set is called the training dataset, which will be used to train the model.
- The second set is called the test dataset or validation set, which will be used to measure the accuracy of the model.
- Sometimes, data is divided into three sets: training, cross-validation, and test. In this case, the test dataset is only used for measuring accuracy, not for training the model (keeping it outside the random split).

3. Train the algorithm with the training dataset. Once an algorithm is trained, it is called a **model**:
    - Model training/creation also involves tuning another parameter called **hyperparameter**. One easy way to understand hyperparameters is to think of them as configuration parameters. Traditionally, hyperparameters are set by hand (hit and trial), but nowadays, there are whole sets of algorithms and methodologies specifically designed for hyperparameter tuning.

4. Use a test dataset to ask another set of questions to the trained algorithm.

The following figure shows a model getting trained by a training dataset:

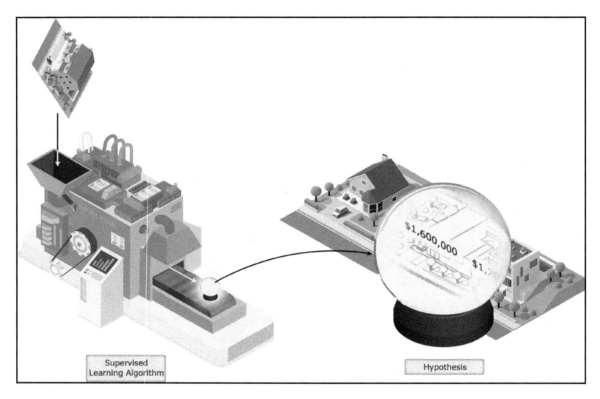

Hypothesis, for what it does, may sound like a misnomer here, and you may think that prediction function may be a better name, but the word hypothesis is used for historic reasons.

If we use only one feature to predict the outcome, it is called **bivariate analysis**. When we have multiple features, it is called **multivariate analysis**. In fact, we can have as many features as we like. One such algorithm, **support vector machines** (**SVM**), which we will cover in the next chapter, allows you to have an infinite number of features.

This chapter covers how to do supervised learning.

 Mathematical explanations have been provided in as simple a way as possible, but you can feel free to skip the math and directly go to the *How to do it...* section.

Using linear regression

Linear regression is the approach to model the value of a response or outcome variable y, based on one or more predictor variables or features, represented by x.

Getting ready

Let's use some housing data to predict the price of a house based on its size. The following are the sizes and prices of houses in the City of Saratoga, CA, in early 2014:

House size (sq. ft.)	Price
2100	**$ 1,620,000**
2300	$ 1,690,000
2046	$ 1,400,000
4314	$ 2,000,000
1244	$ 1,060,000
4608	$ 3,830,000
2173	$ 1,230,000
2750	$ 2,400,000
4010	$ 3,380,000
1959	$ 1,480,000

Here's a graphical representation of the same:

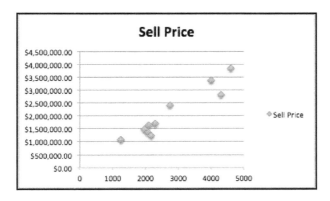

How to do it...

1. Start the Spark shell:

   ```
   $ spark-shell
   ```

2. Import the statistics and related classes:

   ```
   scala> import org.apache.spark.ml.linalg.Vectors
   scala> import org.apache.spark.ml.regression.LinearRegression
   ```

3. Create a DataFrame with the house price as the label:

   ```
   scala>  val points = spark.createDataFrame(Seq(
      (1620000,Vectors.dense(2100)),
      (1690000,Vectors.dense(2300)),
      (1400000,Vectors.dense(2046)),
      (2000000,Vectors.dense(4314)),
      (1060000,Vectors.dense(1244)),
      (3830000,Vectors.dense(4608)),
      (1230000,Vectors.dense(2173)),
      (2400000,Vectors.dense(2750)),
      (3380000,Vectors.dense(4010)),
      (1480000,Vectors.dense(1959))
      )).toDF("label","features")
   ```

4. Initialize linear regression:

   ```
   scala> val lr = new LinearRegression()
   ```

5. Train a model using this data:

   ```
   scala> val model = lr.fit(points)
   ```

5. Create some test data:

   ```
   scala> val test =
   spark.createDataFrame(Seq(Vectors.dense(2100)).map(Tuple1.apply)).t
   oDF("features")
   ```

6. Make predictions for the test data:

   ```
   scala> val predictions = model.transform(test)
   ```

There's more...

House size is just one predictor variable. A house price depends upon other variables, such as the lot size, age of the house, and so on. The more variables you have, the better your prediction will be.

In this recipe, since the dataset is small and we are just getting started, we have just checked the prediction for one vector. In reality, we need to compute the area under the curve and the area under ROC for measuring accuracy.

Let's do the same exercise with more data. The link for this is http://sparkcookbook.amazonaws.com/housingdata/realestate.libsvm.

The data in the preceding link contains housing data for 2,800 houses. Let us repeat the same exercise for the aforementioned dataset:

1. Start the Spark shell:

   ```
   $ spark-shell
   ```

2. Do the necessary imports:

   ```
   scala> import org.apache.spark.ml.regression.LinearRegression
   scala> import org.apache.spark.ml.evaluation.RegressionEvaluator
   ```

3. Load the data in Spark as a dataset:

   ```
   scala> val data =
   spark.read.format("libsvm").load("s3a://sparkcookbook/housingdata/r
   ealestate.libsvm")
   ```

3. Divide the data into training and test datasets:

   ```
   scala> val Array(training, test) = data.randomSplit(Array(0.7,
   0.3))
   ```

4. Instantiate the LinearRegression object:

   ```
   scala> val lr = new LinearRegression()
   ```

5. Fit/train the model:

   ```
   scala> val model = lr.fit(training)
   ```

6. Make predictions on the test dataset:

```scala
scala> val predictions = model.transform(test)
```

7. Instantiate RegressionEvaluator:

```scala
scala> val evaluator = new RegressionEvaluator()
```

8. Evaluate the predictions:

```scala
scala> evaluator.evaluate(predictions)
```

Understanding the cost function

The cost function or loss function is a very important function in machine learning algorithms. Most algorithms have some form of cost function, and the goal is to minimize this. Parameters, which affect cost functions, such as stepSize, are called **hyperparameters**; they need to be set by hand. Therefore, understanding the whole concept of the cost function is very important.

In this recipe, we are going to analyze the cost function in linear regression. Linear regression is a simple algorithm to understand, and it will help you understand the role of cost functions for even complex algorithms.

Let's go back to linear regression. The goal is to find the best-fitting line so that the mean square of the error would be minimum. Here, we are referring to an error as the difference between the value as per the best-fitting line and the actual value of the response variable of the training dataset.

For a simple case of a single predicate variable, the best-fitting line can be written as:

$$y = \theta_0 + \theta_1 x$$

This function is also called the **hypothesis function** and can be written as:

$$h(x) = \theta_0 + \theta_1 x$$

The goal of linear regression is to find the best-fitting line. On this line, θ_0 represents the intercept on the y axis, and θ_1 represents the slope of the line, as is obvious from the following equation:

$$h(x) = \theta_0 + \theta_1 x$$

We have to choose θ_0 and θ_1 in a way that $h(x)$ would be closest to y in the case of the training dataset. So, for the ith data point, the square of the distance between the line and the data point is:

$$\left(x^i - x^i\right)^2 + \left(h\left(x^i\right) - y^i\right)^2$$
$$= \left(h\left(x^i\right) - y^i\right)^2$$

To put it in words, this is the square of the difference between the predicted house price and the actual price the house got sold for. Now, let's take the average of this value across the training dataset:

$$\frac{1}{2m} \sum_{i=1}^{m} \left(h(x)^i - y^i\right)^2$$

The preceding equation is called the cost function J for linear regression. The goal is to minimize this cost function:

$$J(\theta_0, \theta_1) = \frac{1}{2m} \sum_{i=1}^{m} \left(h(x)^i - y^i\right)^2$$

This cost function is also called the **squared error function**. Both θ_0 and θ_1 follow a convex curve independently if they are plotted against J.

Let's take a very simple example of a dataset with three values—*(1,1)*, *(2,2)*, and *(3,3)*—to make the calculation easy:

$$\left(x^1, y^1\right) = \left(1,1\right)$$
$$\left(x^2, y^2\right) = \left(2,2\right)$$
$$\left(x^3, y^3\right) = \left(3,3\right)$$

Let's assume θ_1 is 0, that is, the best-fitting line parallel to the *x* axis. In the first case, assume that the best-fitting line is the *x* axis, that is, *y=0*. In that case, the following will be the value of the cost function:

$$\left(\theta_0, \theta_1\right) = \left(0,0\right)$$
$$J\left(\theta_0\right) = \frac{1}{2 \times 3} \sum_{i=1}^{3} \left(y^i\right)^2$$
$$= \frac{1}{2 \times 3}\left(1 + 4 + 9\right) = \frac{14}{6} = 2.33$$

Move this line up to *y=1*. The following will be the value of the cost function now:

$$\left(\theta_0, \theta_1\right) = \left(1,0\right)$$
$$J\left(\theta_0\right) = \frac{1}{2 \times 3} \sum_{i=1}^{3} \left(1 - y^i\right)^2$$
$$= \frac{1}{2 \times 3}\left(0 + 1 + 4\right) = \frac{5}{6} = 0.83$$

Now let's move this line further up to *y=2*. Then, the following will be the value of the cost function:

$$\left(\theta_0, \theta_1\right) = \left(2, 0\right)$$

$$J\left(\theta_0\right) = \frac{1}{2 \times 3} \sum_{i=1}^{3} \left(2 - y^i\right)^2$$

$$= \frac{1}{2 \times 3} \left(1 + 0 + 1\right) = \frac{2}{6} = 0.33$$

When we move this line further up to *y=3*, the following will be the value of the cost function:

$$\left(\theta_0, \theta_1\right) = \left(3, 0\right)$$

$$J\left(\theta_0\right) = \frac{1}{2 \times 3} \sum_{i=1}^{3} \left(3 - y^i\right)^2$$

$$= \frac{1}{2 \times 3} \left(4 + 1 + 0\right) = \frac{5}{6} = 0.83$$

When we move this line further up to *y=4*, the following will be the value of the cost function:

$$\left(\theta_0, \theta_1\right) = \left(4, 0\right)$$

$$J\left(\theta_0\right) = \frac{1}{2 \times 3} \sum_{i=1}^{3} \left(4 - y^i\right)^2$$

$$= \frac{1}{2 \times 3} \left(9 + 4 + 1\right) = \frac{14}{6} = 2.33$$

So, you saw that the value of the cost function first decreased and then increased again like this:

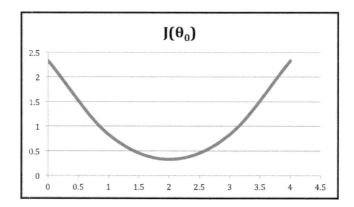

Now let's repeat the exercise by making θ_0 as 0 and using different values of θ_1.

In the first case, assume the best-fitting line is the x axis, that is, $y=0$. The following will be the value of the cost function in this scenario:

$$(\theta_0, \theta_1) = (0, 0)$$

$$J(\theta_1) = \frac{1}{2 \times 3} \sum_{i=1}^{3} (y^i)^2$$

$$= \frac{1}{2 \times 3}(1 + 4 + 9) = \frac{14}{6} = 2.33$$

Use a slope of 0.5. The following will be the value of the cost function now:

$$(\theta_0, \theta_1) = (0, 0.5)$$

$$J(\theta_1) = \frac{1}{2 \times 3} \sum_{i=1}^{3} (0.5x^i - y^i)^2$$

$$= \frac{1}{2 \times 3}(0.25 + 0 + 2.25) = \frac{2.5}{6} = 0.41$$

Now use a slope of *1*. The following will be the value of the cost function:

$$(\theta_0, \theta_1) = (0,1)$$

$$J(\theta_1) = \frac{1}{2 \times 3} \sum_{i=1}^{3} (x^i - y^i)^2$$

$$= \frac{1}{2 \times 3}(0 + 0 + 0) = 0$$

When you use a slope of *1.5*, the following will be the value of the cost function:

$$(\theta_0, \theta_1) = (0, 1.5)$$

$$J(\theta_1) = \frac{1}{2 \times 3} \sum_{i=1}^{3} (1.5x^i - y^i)^2$$

$$= \frac{1}{2 \times 3}(0.25 + 1 + 2.25) = \frac{3.5}{6} = 0.58$$

When you use a slope of *2.0*, the following will be the value of the cost function:

$$(\theta_0, \theta_1) = (0, 2.0)$$

$$J(\theta_1) = \frac{1}{2 \times 3} \sum_{i=1}^{3} (2x^i - y^i)^2$$

$$= \frac{1}{2 \times 3}(1 + 4 + 9) = \frac{14}{6} = 2.33$$

As you can see, in both the graphs, the minimum value of *J* is when the slope or gradient of the curve is *0*:

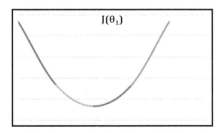

When both θ_0 and θ_1 are mapped to a 3D space, it becomes like the shape of a bowl with the minimum value of the cost function at the bottom of it.

This approach to arrive at the minimum value is called **gradient descent**. In Spark, the implementation is referred to as this: **stochastic gradient descent**.

There's more...

Gradient descent is part of a larger family of optimization techniques called **hill climbing algorithms**. Another noteworthy algorithm in this family, which is used extensively in Spark, is called **Limited-memory BFGS** (**LBFGS**). These algorithms seek a stationary point of a function where the gradient is zero.

Doing linear regression with lasso

Lasso is a shrinkage and selection method for linear regression. It minimizes the usual sum of squared errors with an upper bound on the sum of the absolute values of the coefficients. It is based on the original lasso paper found at http://statweb.stanford.edu/~tibs/lasso/lasso.pdf.

The least square method we used in the last recipe is also called **ordinary least squares** (**OLS**). OLS has two challenges:

- **Prediction accuracy**: Predictions made using OLS usually have low forecast bias and high variance. Prediction accuracy can be improved by shrinking some coefficients (or even making them zero). There will be some increase in bias, but the overall prediction accuracy will improve.
- **Interpretation**: As a large number of predictors are available, it is desirable that we find a subset of them that exhibits the strongest effect (correlation).

Bias versus variance

There are two primary reasons behind a prediction error: bias and variance. The best way to understand bias and variance is to look at a case where we are doing predictions on the same dataset multiple times. Bias is an estimate of how far the predicted results are from the actual values, and variance is an estimate of the difference in predicted values among different predictions. Generally, adding more features helps reduce bias, as can be understood easily.

If, while building a prediction model, we leave out some features with significant correlation, it would lead to a significant error. If your model has high variance, you can remove features to reduce it. A bigger dataset also helps reduce variance.

Here, we are going to use a simple dataset that is ill-posed. An ill-posed dataset is a dataset where the sample data size is smaller than the number of predictors, as shown here:

y	x0	x1	x2	x3	x4	x5	x6	x7	x8
1	5	3	1	2	1	3	2	2	1
2	9	8	8	9	7	9	8	7	9

You can easily guess that out of the nine predictors, only two have a strong correlation with y: x0 and x1. We will use this dataset with the lasso algorithm to see its validity.

How to do it...

1. Start the Spark shell:

   ```
   $ spark-shell
   ```

2. Import the statistics and related classes:

   ```
   scala> import org.apache.spark.ml.linalg.Vectors
   scala> import org.apache.spark.ml.regression.LinearRegression
   ```

3. Create the dataset with the value we created earlier:

   ```
   scala>   val points = spark.createDataFrame(Seq(
       (1d,Vectors.dense(5,3,1,2,1,3,2,2,1)),
       (2d,Vectors.dense(9,8,8,9,7,9,8,7,9))
   )).toDF("label","features")
   ```

4. Initialize the linear regression estimator with elastic net param 1 (means lasso or L1 regularization):

   ```
   scala> val lr = new
   LinearRegression().setMaxIter(10).setRegParam(.3).setFitIntercept(f
   alse).setElasticNetParam(1.0)
   ```

5. Train a model:

   ```
   scala> val model = lr.fit(points)
   ```

6. Check how many predictors have their coefficients set to zero:

```
scala> model.coefficients
   org.apache.spark.ml.linalg.Vector =
[0.17372423795367625,0.025461270520367753,0.0,0.0,0.0,0.01558549706
4731741,0.0,0.0,0.0]
```

As you can see, six out of the nine predictors have got their coefficients set to zero. This is the primary feature of lasso: any predictor it thinks is not useful, it literally moves them out of the equation by setting their coefficients to *zero*.

Doing ridge regression

An alternate way to improve prediction quality is to do ridge regression. In lasso, a lot of the features get their coefficients set to zero and, therefore, eliminated from the equation. In ridge, predictors or features are penalized, but never set to zero. How to do it...

1. Start the Spark shell:

   ```
   $ spark-shell
   ```

2. Import the statistics and related classes:

   ```
   scala> import org.apache.spark.ml.linalg.Vectors
   scala> import org.apache.spark.ml.regression.LinearRegression
   ```

3. Create the dataset with the value we created earlier:

```
scala>  val points = spark.createDataFrame(Seq(
    (1d,Vectors.dense(5,3,1,2,1,3,2,2,1)),
    (2d,Vectors.dense(9,8,8,9,7,9,8,7,9))
)).toDF("label","features")
```

4. Initialize the linear regression estimator with elastic net param 1 (means ridge or L2 regularization):

   ```
   scala> val lr = new
   LinearRegression().setMaxIter(10).setRegParam(.3).setFitIntercept(f
   alse).setElasticNetParam(0.0)
   ```

5. Train a model:

   ```
   scala> val model = lr.fit(points)
   ```

6. Check how many predictors have their coefficients set to zero:

```
scala> model.coefficients
  org.apache.spark.ml.linalg.Vector =
[0.1132933163345012,0.039370733000466666,0.002369276442275222,
  0.01041698759881142,0.004328988574203182,0.026236646722551202,
  0.015282817648377045,0.023597219133656675,0.0011928984792447484]
```

As you can see, unlike lasso, ridge regression does not assign any predictor coefficients the value zero, but it does assign some very close to zero.

8
Supervised Learning with MLlib — Classification

This chapter is divided into the following recipes:

- Doing classification using logistic regression
- Doing binary classification using SVM
- Doing classification using decision trees
- Doing classification using random forest
- Doing classification using gradient boosted trees
- Doing classification with Naïve Bayes

Introduction

The classification problem is like the regression problem discussed in the previous chapter, except that the outcome variable y takes only a few discrete values. In binary classification, y takes only two values: 0 or 1. You can also think of the values that the response variable takes in classification as a representation of categories.

Doing classification using logistic regression

In classification, the response variable y has discreet values as opposed to continuous values. Some examples are e-mail (spam/non-spam), transactions (safe/fraudulent), and so on.

The *y* variable can take two values, namely *0* or *1*, as illustrated in the following equation:

$$y \in \{0,1\}$$

Here, *0* is referred to as a **negative class** and *1* means a **positive class**. Though we are calling them positive or negative, it is only for convenience's sake. Algorithms are neutral about this assignment. Algorithms have no emotions, and *1* does not mean higher than or better than *0*.

Though linear regression works well with regression tasks, it hits a few limitations when it comes to classification tasks. These include:

- The fitting process is very susceptible to outliers
- There is no guarantee that the hypothesis function *h(x)* will fit in the range of *0* (negative class) to *1* (positive class)

Logistic regression guarantees that *h(x)* will fit between *0* and *1*. Though logistic regression has the word "regression" in it, it is more of a misnomer; it is very much a classification algorithm:

$$1 \geq h(x) \geq 0$$

In linear regression, the hypothesis function is as follows:

$$h(x) = \theta^T x$$

In logistic regression, we slightly modify the hypothesis equation like this:

$$h(x) = g\left(\theta^T x\right)$$

The *g* function is called the **sigmoid function** or **logistic function** and is defined for a real number *t* as follows:

$$g(t) = \frac{1}{1 + e^{-t}}$$

This is how the sigmoid function appears as a graph:

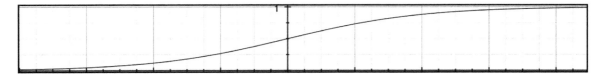

As you can see, when t approaches negative infinity, $g(t)$ approaches 0; likewise, when t approaches infinity, $g(t)$ approaches 1. This guarantees that the hypothesis function's output will never fall out of the 0 to 1 range.

Now the hypothesis function can be rewritten as:

$$h(x) = \frac{1}{1 + e^{-\theta^T x}}$$

Here, $h(x)$ is the estimated probability indicating that y equals 1 for a given predictor x; therefore, $h(x)$ can also be rewritten as:

$$h(x) = P(y = 1 \mid x; \theta)$$

In other words, the hypothesis function is showing the probability of y being 1, given the feature matrix x, parameterized by θ. This probability can be any real number between 0 and 1, but our goal of classification does not allow us to have continuous values; we can only have two values—0 or 1—to indicate either the negative or positive class.

Let's say that we predict $y = 1$ if $h(x) \geq 0.5$ and $y = 0$. If you look at the sigmoid function graph again, you will realize that when the $t \geq 0$ sigmoid function is ≥ 0.5, that is, for positive values of t, it will predict the positive class:

$$h(x) = g\left(\theta^T x\right)$$

This means for $\theta^T x \geq 0$, the positive class will be predicted. To better illustrate this, let's expand it to a non-matrix form for a bivariate case:

$$\theta^T x \geq 0$$
$$\theta_0 x_0 + \theta_1 x_1 + \theta_2 x_2 \geq 0$$

The plane represented by the equation $\theta_0 x_0 + \theta_1 x_1 + \theta_2 x_2 = 0$ will decide whether a given vector belongs to the positive or negative class. This line is called the **decision boundary**.

This boundary does not have to be linear depending on the training set. If the training data does not separate between positive and negative sets across a linear decision boundary, high-level polynomial features can be added to facilitate it. An example can be to add two new features by squaring x_1 and x_2, as follows:

$$h(x) = \theta_0 x_0 + \theta_1 x_1 + \theta_2 x_2 + \theta_3 x_1^2 + \theta_4 x_2^2$$

Note that to the learning algorithm, this enhancement is exactly the same as the following equation:

$$h(x) = \theta_0 x_0 + \theta_1 x_1 + \theta_2 x_2 + \theta_3 x_3 + \theta_4 x_4$$

The learning algorithm will treat the introduction of polynomials as just another feature. This gives you great power when dealing with the fitting process. It means any complex decision boundary can be created with the right choice of polynomials and parameters.

Let's spend some time trying to understand how to choose the right value for the parameters, like we did in the case of linear regression. The cost function J in the case of linear regression was:

$$J(\theta_0, \theta_1) = \frac{1}{2m} \sum_{i=1}^{m} \left(h(x^i) - y^i \right)^2$$

As you know, we are averaging the cost of this cost function. Let's represent this in terms of a cost term:

$$Cost\left(h(x^i) - y^i \right) = \frac{\left(h(x^i) - y^i \right)^2}{2}$$

$$J(\theta_0, \theta_1) = \frac{1}{m} \sum_{i=1}^{m} Cost\left(h(x^i) - y^i \right)$$

In other words, the cost term is the cost the algorithm has to pay if it predicts *h(x)* for a real response variable value *y*:

$$Cost\left(h\left(x\right)-y\right)=\frac{\left(h\left(x\right)-y\right)^{2}}{2}$$

This cost works fine for linear regression, but for logistic regression, this cost function is non-convex (that is, it leads to multiple local minimums), and we need to find a better way to estimate the cost.

Cost functions that work well with logistic regression are as follows:

$$Cost\left(h\left(x\right),y\right)=-\log\left(h\left(x\right)\right)//\text{for positive class}$$
$$Cost\left(h\left(x\right),y\right)=-\log\left(1-h\left(x\right)\right)//\text{for negative class}$$

Let's put these two cost functions into one by combining the two:

$$Cost\left(h\left(x\right),y\right)=-y\log\left(h\left(x\right)\right)-\left(1-y\right)\log\left(1-h\left(x\right)\right)$$

Let's put this cost function back to *J*:

$$J\left(\theta\right)=-\frac{1}{m}\sum_{i=1}^{m}\left(y^{i}\log h\left(x^{i}\right)+\left(1-y^{i}\right)\log\left(1-h\left(x^{i}\right)\right)\right)$$

The goal would be to minimize the cost, that is, minimize the value of *J(θ)*. You can do this using the gradient descent algorithm. Spark MLLib has two classes that support logistic regression:

- `LogisticRegressionWithSGD`
- `LogisticRegressionWithLBFGS`

Both **Stochastic Gradient Descent (SGD)** and the **Limited Broyden-Fletcher-Goldfarb-Shanno (LBFGS)** algorithm are part of hill climbing algorithms. We have seen in the previous chapters that SGD requires the tuning of two hyperparameters: step size and the number of steps. LBFGS does this hyperparameter tuning automatically.

Spark ML has only one `LogisticRegression` library.

Getting ready

In 2006, Suzuki, Tsurusaki, and Kodama did some research on the distribution of an endangered burrowing spider on different beaches in Japan. Refer to `https://www.jstage.jst.go.jp/article/asjaa/55/2/55_2_79/_pdf` for more information.

Here's some data about the grain size and the presence of the spiders:

Grain size (mm)	Spider present
0.245	**Absent**
0.247	Absent
0.285	Present
0.299	Present
0.327	Present
0.347	Present
0.356	Absent
0.36	Present
0.363	Absent
0.364	Present
0.398	Absent
0.4	Present
0.409	Absent
0.421	Present
0.432	Absent
0.473	Present
0.509	Present
0.529	Present
0.561	Absent
0.569	Absent
0.594	Present
0.638	Present

Grain size (mm)	Spider present
0.656	Present
0.816	Present
0.853	Present
0.938	Present
1.036	Present
1.045	Present

We will use this data to train the algorithm. The result *Absent* will be denoted by 0 and *Present* by 1.

How to do it...

1. Start the Spark shell:

   ```
   $ spark-shell
   ```

2. Import the statistics and related classes:

   ```scala
   scala> import org.apache.spark.ml.classification.
   {BinaryLogisticRegressionSummary, LogisticRegression}
   scala> import org.apache.spark.ml.linalg.{Vector, Vectors}
   ```

3. Create a dataset with either the presence or absence of spiders as the label:

   ```scala
   scala>  val trainingDataSet = spark.createDataFrame(Seq(
   (0.0,Vectors.dense(0.245)),
   (0.0,Vectors.dense(0.247)),
   (1.0,Vectors.dense(0.285)),
   (1.0,Vectors.dense(0.299)),
   (1.0,Vectors.dense(0.327)),
   (1.0,Vectors.dense(0.347)),
   (0.0,Vectors.dense(0.356)),
   (1.0,Vectors.dense(0.36)),
   (0.0,Vectors.dense(0.363)),
   (1.0,Vectors.dense(0.364)),
   (0.0,Vectors.dense(0.398)),
   (1.0,Vectors.dense(0.4)),
   (0.0,Vectors.dense(0.409)),
   (1.0,Vectors.dense(0.421)),
   (0.0,Vectors.dense(0.432)),
   ```

```
(1.0,Vectors.dense(0.473)),
(1.0,Vectors.dense(0.509)),
(1.0,Vectors.dense(0.529)),
(0.0,Vectors.dense(0.561)),
(0.0,Vectors.dense(0.569)),
(1.0,Vectors.dense(0.594)),
(1.0,Vectors.dense(0.638)),
(1.0,Vectors.dense(0.656)),
(1.0,Vectors.dense(0.816)),
(1.0,Vectors.dense(0.853)),
(1.0,Vectors.dense(0.938)),
(1.0,Vectors.dense(1.036)),
(1.0,Vectors.dense(1.045)))).toDF("label","features")
```

4. Train a model using this data:

```
scala> val lr = new LogisticRegression
scala> val model = lr.fit(trainingDataSet)
```

5. Create `model.summary`:

```
scala> val trainingSummary = model.summary
```

6. Cast it as an instance of the binomial logistic regression summary:

```
scala> val binarySummary =
trainingSummary.asInstanceOf[BinaryLogisticRegressionSummary]
```

7. Print the area under **Receiver Operating Characteristic (ROC)**:

```
scala> println(s"areaUnderROC: ${binarySummary.areaUnderROC}")
```

There's more...

What happened to all the grunt work which was supposed to be done before finding the area under the curve and area under ROC? The underlying process is still the same, that is:

1. Get the labeled data.
2. Divide it into training and test or validation sets.
3. Train the algorithm using the training set.
4. Validate it using the test set.
5. Report its accuracy using the area under the curve/ROC.

In this case, the libraries did the process automatically.

What is ROC?

ROC is a statistical tool to assess the accuracy of predictions. The accuracy of predictions plays a major role in how predictions would be used.

Quoting Prof. Andrew Ng, Stanford University, chief scientist at Baidu, here for reference:

> *"The difference between 95% accuracy versus 99% accuracy is between you sometimes making use of it versus using it all the time ."*

ROC curves provide a visually appealing way to summarize the accuracy of predictions.

Doing binary classification using SVM

Classification is a technique to put data into different classes based on its utility. For example, an e-commerce company can apply two labels, namely *will buy* or *will not buy*, to the potential visitors.

This classification is done by providing some already labeled data to machine-learning algorithms called **training data**, as you know already. The challenge is how to mark the boundary between the two classes. Let's take a simple example, as shown in the following figure:

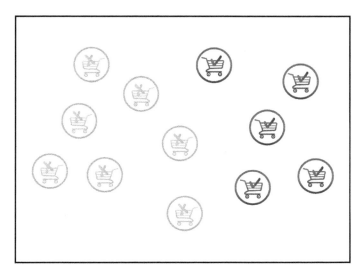

In the preceding case, we designated **gray** and **black** to the "will not buy" and "will buy" labels, respectively. Here, drawing a line between the two classes is easy, as follows:

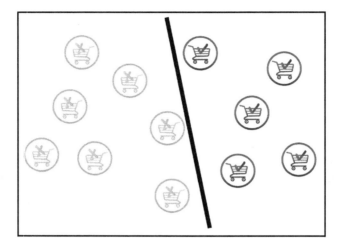

Is this the best we can do? Not really. Let's try to do a better job. The black classifier is not really equidistant from the will buy and will not buy carts. Let's make a better attempt:

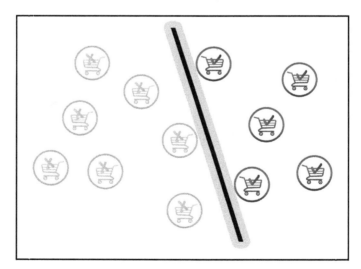

This looks good, doesn't it? This, in fact, is what the SVM algorithm does. You can see in the preceding diagram that there are only three carts that decide the slope of the line: two black carts above the line and one gray cart below the line. These carts are called **support vectors**, and the rest of the carts, that is, the vectors, are irrelevant.

Sometimes it's not easy to draw a line and a curve may be needed to separate two classes, such as the following:

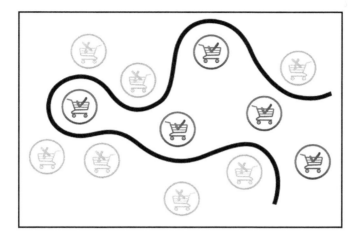

Sometimes, even that is not enough. In such cases, we need more than two dimensions to resolve the problem. Rather than a classified line, what we need is a hyperplane. In fact, whenever data is too cluttered, adding extra dimensions will help you find a hyperplane to separate the classes. The following diagram illustrates this:

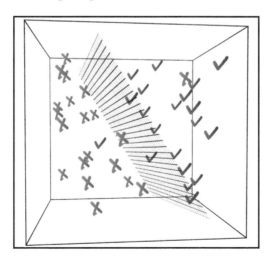

This does not mean that adding extra dimensions is always a good idea. Most of the time, our goal is to reduce dimensions and keep only the relevant dimensions/features. A whole set of algorithms is dedicated to dimensionality reduction; we will cover them in later chapters.

Getting ready

In this recipe, we are going to use the **Pima Indians Diabetes Database**. This database is owned by the *National Institute of Diabetes and Digestive and Kidney Diseases*. The original CSV files contain features in the following order:

- Number of times pregnant
- Plasma glucose concentration at 2 hours in an oral glucose tolerance test
- Diastolic blood pressure (mmHg)
- Triceps skinfold thickness (mm)
- 2-hour serum insulin (mu U/ml)
- Body mass index (weight in kg/(height in m^2)
- Diabetes pedigree function
- Age (years)
- Class variable (0 or 1)

The ninth value here is the label that tells whether the given person has diabetes or not. For your convenience, the CSV file is loaded in the following public s3 location: http://sparkc ookbook.s3.amazonaws.com/medicaldata/diabetes.csv.

Data has also been converted into libsvm and loaded at http://sparkcookbook.s3.amazo naws.com/medicaldata/diabetes.libsvm.

How to do it...

1. Start the Spark shell:

   ```
   $ spark-shell
   ```

2. Do the required imports:

   ```
   scala> import org.apache.spark.mllib.util.MLUtils
   scala> import org.apache.spark.mllib.classification.SVMWithSGD
   ```

3. Load the data as an RDD:

   ```
   scala> val data =
   MLUtils.loadLibSVMFile(sc,"s3a://sparkcookbook
   /medicaldata/diabetes.libsvm")
   ```

4. Count the number of records:

```scala
scala> data.count
```

5. Divide the dataset into equal halves of training data and testing data:

```scala
scala> val trainingAndTest = data.randomSplit(Array(0.5,0.5))
```

6. Assign the `training` and `test` data:

```scala
scala> val trainingData = trainingAndTest(0)
scala> val testData = trainingAndTest(1)
```

7. Train the algorithm and build the model for 100 iterations (you can try different iterations, but at a certain point of inflection , you'll see that the results start to converge and that point of inflection is the right number of iterations to choose):

```scala
scala> val model = SVMWithSGD.train(trainingData,100)
```

8. Now you can use this model to predict a label for any dataset. Predict the label for the first point in the test data:

```scala
scala> val label = model.predict(testData.first.features)
```

9. Create a tuple that has the first value as a prediction for the test data and the second value as the actual label, which will help us compute the accuracy of our algorithm:

```scala
scala> val predictionsAndLabels = testData.map( r =>
(model.predict(r.features),r.label))
```

10. You can count how many records have predictions and actual label mismatches:

```scala
scala> predictionsAndLabels.filter(p => p._1 != p._2).count
```

Doing classification using decision trees

Decision trees are the most intuitive among machine-learning algorithms. We use decision trees in our daily lives all the time.

Decision tree algorithms have a lot of useful features:

- Easy to understand and interpret
- Work with both categorical and continuous features

- Work with missing features
- Do not require feature scaling

Decision tree algorithms work in an upside-down order in which an expression containing a feature is evaluated at every level and this splits the dataset into two categories. We will help you understand this with a simple dumb charades example, which most of us may have played in college. I guessed an animal and asked my coworker to ask me questions to work out my choice. Here's how her questioning went:

- Q1: Is it a big animal?

    Answer: Yes.

- Q2: Does this animal live for more than 40 years?

    Answer: Yes.

- Q3: Is this animal an elephant?

    Answer: Yes.

This is obviously an oversimplified case in which she knew I had postulated an elephant (what else would you guess in a big data world?). Let's expand this example to include some more animals, as in the following figure (dark grayed boxes are classes):

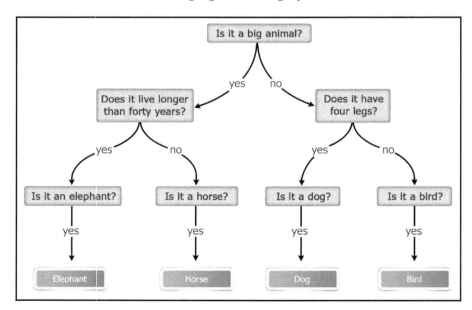

The preceding example is a case of multinomial classification. In this recipe, we are going to focus on binomial classification.

Getting ready

Whenever someone has to take tennis lessons in the morning, the night before, the instructor checks the weather report and decides whether the next morning would be good to play tennis. This recipe will use this as an example to build a decision tree.

Let's decide on the features of weather that affect the decision whether to play tennis in the morning or not:

- Rain
- Wind speed
- Temperature

Let's build a table using different combinations of these features:

Rain	Windy	Temperature	Play tennis?
Yes	Yes	Hot	No
Yes	Yes	Normal	No
Yes	Yes	Cool	No
No	Yes	Hot	No
No	Yes	Cool	No
No	No	Hot	Yes
No	No	Normal	Yes
No	No	Cool	No

Now how do we build a decision tree? We can start with one of the three features: rain, wind speed, or temperature. The rule is to start in such a way that maximum **information gain** would be possible.

Information gain means identifying the fastest way to reach a decision. In fact, it is a concept that we use in everyday life. Being a busy executive, I get hundreds of e-mails every day. We get a mix of spam and important client inquiries in the same e-mail stream. So no e-mail can be ignored without being processed. My goal while processing e-mails is to maximize information gain. The action item for me in this case is to determine whether I'm looking for information or an outcome. I start with the subject and then proceed to the first few lines. By this time, I have an idea about what needs to be done with the e-mail: for example, send a quick reply, forward/delegate it, star it for later processing, mark as spam, block the sender, and so on. Every now and then, I get e-mails that are complete essays, but due to the inefficiency of information gain, they get ignored.

On a rainy day, as you can see in the table, other features do not matter and there is no play. The same is true for high wind velocity.

Decision trees, like most other algorithms, take feature values only as double values. So let's do the mapping:

$$Rain\{Yes, No\} => \{2.0, 1.0\}$$
$$Windy\{Yes, No\} => \{2.0, 1.0\}$$
$$Temperature\{Hot, Normal, Cold\} => \{3.0, 2.0, 1.0\}$$

The positive class is *1.0* and the negative class is *0.0*. Let's load the data using the CSV format, with the first value as a label:

```
$ vi tennis.csv
0.0,1.0,1.0,2.0
0.0,1.0,1.0,1.0
0.0,1.0,1.0,0.0
0.0,0.0,1.0,2.0
0.0,0.0,1.0,0.0
1.0,0.0,0.0,2.0
1.0,0.0,0.0,1.0
0.0,0.0,0.0,0.0
```

How to do it...

1. Start the Spark shell:

```
$ spark-shell
```

2. Perform the required imports:

```
scala> import org.apache.spark.mllib.tree.DecisionTree
scala> import org.apache.spark.mllib.regression.LabeledPoint
scala> import org.apache.spark.mllib.linalg.Vectors
scala> import org.apache.spark.mllib.tree.configuration.Algo._
scala> import org.apache.spark.mllib.tree.impurity.Entropy
```

3. Load the file:

```
scala> val data = sc.textFile("tennis.csv")
```

4. Parse the data and load it into `LabeledPoint`:

```
scala>  val parsedData = data.map {
line =>  val parts = line.split(',').map(_.toDouble)
 LabeledPoint(parts(0), Vectors.dense(parts.tail)) }
```

5. Train the algorithm with this data:

```
scala> val model = DecisionTree.train(parsedData,
Classification, Entropy, 3)
```

6. Create a vector for no rain, high wind, and cool temperature:

```
scala> val v=Vectors.dense(0.0,1.0,0.0)
```

7. Predict whether tennis should be played:

```
scala> model.predict(v)
```

How it works...

Let's draw a decision tree for the tennis example we created in this recipe:

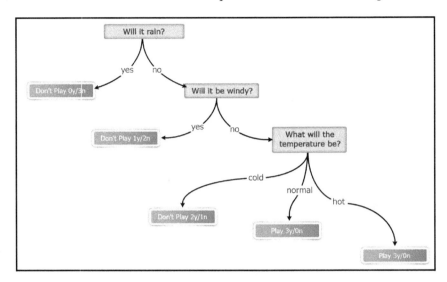

This model has a depth of three levels. Which attribute to select depends upon how we can maximize information gain. We compute this by measuring the purity of the split. Purity means that irrespective of whether the certainty of playing tennis is increasing, the given dataset will be considered positive or negative. In this example, this equates to whether the chances of play are increasing or the chances of not playing are increasing.

Purity is measured using **entropy**. Entropy is a measure of disorder in a system. In this context, it is easier to understand it as a measure of uncertainty:

$$Entropy(S) = -p + log_2 p + -p - log_2 p -$$

The highest level of purity is *0* and the lowest is *1*. Let's try to determine purity, in this case, using a formula.

When rain is *yes*, the probability of playing tennis is *p+*, which is *0/3 = 0*. The probability of not playing tennis is *p-*, which is *3/3 = 1*:

$$Entropy(S) = -0 - 1log1 = 0$$

This is a pure set.

When rain is *no*, the probability of playing tennis is *p+*, which is *2/5 = 0.4*. The probability of not playing tennis is *p-*, which is *3/5 = 0.6*:

$$Entropy(S) = -0.4log_2 04 - 0.6log_2 0.6$$
$$= -0.4 \times (-1.32) - 0.6 \times (-0.736)$$
$$= 0.528 + 0.4416$$
$$= 0.967$$

This is almost an impure set. The most impure would be the case where the probability is *0.5*.

Spark uses three measures to determine impurity:

- Gini impurity (classification)
- Entropy (classification)
- Variance (regression)

Information gain is the difference between the parent node impurity and the weighted sum of two child node impurities. Let's look at the first split, which partitions data of size *8* into two datasets of size *3* (left) and *5* (right). Let's call the first split *s1*, the parent node *rain*, the left child *no rain*, and the right child *wind*. So the information gain would be:

$$IG(rain, s1) = Impurity(rain) - \left(\frac{N_{no\ rain}}{N_{rain}}\right) Impurity(no\ rain)$$
$$- \left(\frac{N_{wind}}{N_{rain}}\right) Impurity(wind)$$

As we have already calculated the impurity for *no rain* and *wind* for the entropy, let's calculate the entropy for *rain*:

$$Entropy(rain) = -\left(\frac{2}{8}\right)log_2\left(\frac{2}{8}\right) - \left(\frac{6}{8}\right)log_2\left(\frac{6}{8}\right)$$
$$= -\left(\frac{1}{4}\right) \times (-2) - \left(\frac{3}{4}\right) \times (-0.41)$$
$$= 0.8$$

Let's calculate the information gain now:

$$IG(rain, s1) = Impurity(rain) - \left(\frac{N_{no\ rain}}{N_{rain}}\right) Impurity(no\ rain)$$
$$- \left(\frac{N_{wind}}{N_{rain}}\right) Impurity(wind)$$
$$= 0.8 - \left(\frac{5}{8}\right) \times 0.967$$
$$= 0.2$$

So the information gain is *0.2* in the first split. Is this the best we can achieve? Let's see what our algorithm comes up with. First, let's find out the depth of the tree:

```scala
scala> model.depth
Int = 2
```

Here, the depth is 2 compared to 3, which we have built intuitively, so this model seems to be better optimized. Let's look at the structure of the tree:

```scala
scala> model.toDebugString
String = "DecisionTreeModel classifier of depth 2 with 5 nodes
If (feature 1 <= 0.0)
   If (feature 2 <= 0.0)
      Predict: 0.0
   Else (feature 2 > 0.0)
      Predict: 1.0
Else (feature 1 > 0.0)
      Predict: 0.0
```

Let's build it visually to get a better understanding:

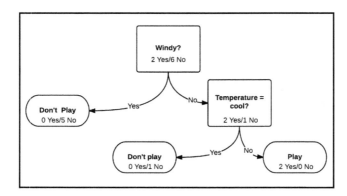

We will not go into detail here, as we have already done this in the previous model. We will straightaway calculate the information gain:

$$IG_{windy?}, s1 = Impurity_{windy?} - N_{no\ wind} N_{windy?} Impurity(no\ wind)$$
$$- N_{windy} N_{windy?} Impurity(windy)$$
$$= 0.44$$

As you can see, in this case, the information gain is *0.44*, which is more than double of the first model.

If you look at the second level nodes, the impurity is zero. In this case, it is great as we got it at a depth of 2. Imagine a situation in which the depth is 50. In that case, the decision tree would work well for training data and would do badly for test data. This situation is called **overfitting**.

One solution to avoid overfitting is **pruning**. You divide your training data into two sets: the training set and validation set. You train the model using the training set. Now you test with the model against the validation set by slowly removing the left nodes. If removing the leaf node (which is mostly a singleton, that is, it contains only one data point) improves the performance of the model, then the leaf node is pruned from the model.

There's more...

Let's apply the decision tree to the diabetes dataset we worked on in the previous recipe:

1. Start the Spark shell or the *Databricks Cloud* shell and do the necessary imports:

```
$ spark-shell
scala> import
org.apache.spark.ml.classification.DecisionTreeClassifier
scala> import
org.apache.spark.ml.evaluation.BinaryClassificationEvaluator
```

2. Read the diabetes data as a DataFrame:

```
scala> val data =
spark.read.format("libsvm").option("inferschema","true")
.load("s3a://sparkcookbook/medicaldata/diabetes.libsvm")
```

3. Split it into `training` and `test` datasets:

```scala
scala> val Array(trainingData, testData) =
data.randomSplit(Array(0.7, 0.3))
```

4. Initialize the decision tree classifier:

```scala
scala> val dt = new DecisionTreeClassifier()
```

5. Train the model using the `training` data:

```scala
scala> val model = dt.fit(trainingData)
```

6. Do predictions on the `test` dataset:

```scala
scala> val predictions = model.transform(testData)
```

7. Initialize the evaluator:

```scala
scala> val evaluator = new BinaryClassificationEvaluator()
```

8. Evaluate the predictions:

```scala
scala> val auroc = evaluator.evaluate(predictions)
```

9. Print the area under the curve:

```scala
scala> println(s"Area under ROC = $auroc")
Area under ROC = 0.7624556737588652
```

We used the decision tree classifier here without tweaking a hyperparameter and got 76 percent of the area under the curve. Why don't you tweak hyperparameters yourselves and see whether you can improve it even further?

Doing classification using random forest

Sometimes, one decision tree is not enough, so a set of decision trees is used to produce more powerful models. These are called **ensemble learning algorithms**. Ensemble learning algorithms are not limited to using decision trees as base models.

The most popular ensemble learning algorithm is **random forest**. In random forest, rather than growing one single tree, *K number of* trees are grown. Every tree is given a random subset *S* of training data. To add a twist to it, every tree only uses a subset of features. When it comes to making predictions, a majority vote is done on the trees and that becomes the prediction.

Let me explain this with an example. The goal is to make a prediction for a given person about whether he/she has good credit or bad credit.

To do this, we will provide labeled training data—in this case, a person with features and labels indicating whether he/she has good credit or bad credit. Now we do not want to create feature bias, so we will provide a randomly selected set of features. There is another reason to provide a randomly selected subset of features: most real-world data has hundreds, if not thousands, of features. Text classification algorithms, for example, typically have *50k-100k* features.

In this case, to add flavor to the story, we are not going to provide features, but we will ask different people why they think a person has good or bad credit. Now, by definition, different people are exposed to the different features (sometimes overlapping) of a person, which gives us the same functionality as randomly selected features.

Our first example features **Jack,** who carries a *bad credit* label. We start with **Joey**, who works at Jack's favorite bar, the Elephant Bar. The only way a person can deduce why a label is given to an individual is by asking yes/no questions. Let's see what Joey says:

- Question 1: Does Jack tip well? (feature: generosity)

  Answer: No

- Question 2: Does Jack spend at least $60 per visit? (feature: spendthrift)

  Answer: Yes

- Question 3: Does he tend to get into bar fights even at the smallest provocation? (feature: volatile)

  Answer: Yes

That explains why Jack has bad credit.

We now ask Jack's girlfriend, **Stacey**:

- Question 1: When you hang out, does Jack always cover the bill? (feature: generosity)

    Answer: No

- Question 2: Has Jack paid you back the $500 he owes? (feature: responsibility)

    Answer: No

- Question 3: Does he overspend sometimes just to show off? (feature: spendthrift)

    Answer: Yes

That explains why Jack has bad credit.

We now ask Jack's best friend, **George**:

- Question 1: When both you and Jack hang out at your apartment, does he clean up himself? (feature: organized)

    Answer: No

- Question 2: Did Jack arrive empty-handed during the Super Bowl potluck? (feature: care)

    Answer: Yes

- Question 3: Has he used the *"I forgot my wallet at home"* excuse for you to cover his tab at restaurants? (feature: responsibility)

    Answer: Yes

That explains why Jack has bad credit.

Now we talk about **Jessica** who has good credit. Let's ask Stacey, who happens to be Jessica's sister:

- Question 1: Whenever you run short of money, does Jessica offer help? (feature: generosity)

    Answer: Yes

- Question 2: Does Jessica pay her bills on time? (feature: responsibility)

    Answer: Yes

- Question 3: Does Jessica offer to babysit your child? (feature: care)

    Answer: Yes

That explains why Jessica has good credit.

Now we ask George who happens to be her husband:

- Question 1: Does Jessica keep the house tidy? (feature: organized)

    Answer: Yes

- Question 2: Does she expect expensive gifts? (feature: spendthrift)

    Answer: No

- Question 3: Does she get upset when you forget to mow the lawn? (feature: volatile)

    Answer: No

That explains why Jessica has good credit.

Now let's ask Joey, the bartender at the Elephant Bar:

- Question 1: Whenever she comes to the bar with friends, is she mostly the designated driver? (feature: responsible)

    Answer: Yes

- Question 2: Does she always take leftovers home? (feature: spendthrift)

    Answer: Yes

- Question 3: Does she tip well? (feature: generosity)

    Answer: Yes

That explains why she has a good credit.

The way random forest works is that it does a random selection on two levels:

- A subset of the data
- A subset of features to split that data

Both these subsets can overlap.

In our example, we have six features and we are going to assign three features to each tree. This way, there is a good chance we will have an overlap.

Let's add eight more people to our `training` dataset:

Names	Label	Generosity	Responsibility	Care	Organization	Spendthrift	Volatile
Jack	0	0	0	0	0	1	1
Jessica	1	1	1	1	1	0	0
Jenny	0	0	0	1	0	1	1
Rick	1	1	1	0	1	0	0
Pat	0	0	0	0	0	1	1
Jeb	1	1	1	1	0	0	0
Jay	1	0	1	1	1	0	0
Nat	0	1	0	0	0	1	1
Ron	1	0	1	1	1	0	0
Mat	0	1	0	0	0	1	1

Getting ready

Let's put the data we created into the `libsvm` format in the following file:

```
rf_libsvm_data.txt
0 5:1 6:1
1 1:1 2:1 3:1 4:1
0 3:1 5:1 6:1
1 1:1 2:1 4:1
0 5:1 6:1
1 1:1 2:1 3:1 4:1
0 1:1 5:1 6:1
1 2:1 3:1 4:1
0 1:1 5:1 6:1
```

This file has been uploaded to S3 for your convenience.

How to do it...

1. Start the Spark shell:

   ```
   $ spark-shell
   ```

2. Perform the required imports:

   ```
   scala> import org.apache.spark.ml.classification.
   {RandomForestClassificationModel,RandomForestClassifier}
   scala> import
   org.apache.spark.ml.evaluation.MulticlassClassificationEvaluator
   ```

3. Load and parse the data:

   ```
   scala> val data =
   spark.read.format("libsvm").load("s3a://sparkcookbook/rf")
   ```

4. Split the data into `training` and `test` datasets:

   ```
   scala> val Array(training, test) = data.randomSplit(Array(0.7,
   0.3))
   ```

5. Create a classification as a tree strategy (random forest also supports regression):

   ```
   scala> val rf = new RandomForestClassifier().setNumTrees(3)
   ```

6. Train the model:

   ```
   scala> val model = rf.fit(training)
   ```

7. Evaluate the model on test instances and compute the test error:

   ```
   scala> val predictions = model.transform(test)
   scala> val evaluator = new
   MulticlassClassificationEvaluator().setMetricName("accuracy")
   scala> val accuracy = evaluator.evaluate(predictions)
   ```

8. Check the model:

   ```
   scala> model.toDebugString
   "RandomForestClassificationModel (uid=rfc_ac46ea5af585) with 3
   trees
   Tree 0 (weight 1.0):
   If (feature 1 <= 0.0)
   Predict: 0.0
   Else (feature 1 > 0.0)
   ```

```
Predict: 1.0
Tree 1 (weight 1.0):
If (feature 5 <= 0.0)
Predict: 1.0
Else (feature 5 > 0.0)
Predict: 0.0
Tree 2 (weight 1.0):
If (feature 5 <= 0.0)
Predict: 1.0
Else (feature 5 > 0.0)
Predict: 0.0
"
```

9. We used toy data to illustrate the value of random forest, but now, let's do the same exercise on the diabetes data by replacing step 3 with the following and running steps 4 to 7 again:

```
scala> val data =
spark.read.format("libsvm").load("s3a://sparkcookbook/patientdata")
```

Now the accuracy has reached 74.6 percent.

Doing classification using gradient boosted trees

Another ensemble learning algorithm is **gradient boosted trees** (**GBTs**). GBTs train one tree at a time, where each new tree improves upon the shortcomings of the previously trained trees.

As GBTs train one tree at a time, they can take longer than random forest.

Getting ready

Let us do GBT on the same patient data and see how the accuracy differs.

How to do it...

1. Start the Spark shell:

```
$ spark-shell
```

2. Perform the required imports:

```
scala> import
org.apache.spark.ml.classification.{GBTClassificationModel,
    GBTClassifier}
scala> import
    org.apache.spark.ml.evaluation.MulticlassClassificationEvaluator
```

3. Load and parse the data:

```
scala> val data =
spark.read.format("libsvm").load("s3a://sparkcookbook/patientdata")
```

4. Split the data into `training` and `test` datasets:

```
scala> val Array(training, test) = data.randomSplit(Array(0.7,
0.3))
```

5. Create a classification as a boosting strategy and set the number of iterations to 3:

```
scala> val gbt = new GBTClassifier().setMaxIter(10)
```

6. Train the model:

```
scala> val model = gbt.fit(training)
```

7. Evaluate the model on the test instances and compute the test error:

```
scala> val predictions = model.transform(test)
scala> val evaluator = new
MulticlassClassificationEvaluator().setMetricName("accuracy")
scala> val accuracy = evaluator.evaluate(predictions)
```

In this case, the accuracy of the model is 75 percent, which is almost the same as what we got for a random forest.

Doing classification with Naïve Bayes

Let's consider building an e-mail spam filter using machine learning. Here we are interested in two classes: spam for unsolicited messages and non-spam for regular e-mails:

$$y \in \{0,1\}$$

The first challenge is that given an e-mail, how do we represent it as feature vector x. An e-mail is just a bunch of text or a collection of words (therefore, this problem domain falls into a broader category called **text classification**). Let's represent an e-mail with a feature vector with the length equal to the size of the dictionary. If a given word in a dictionary appears in an e-mail, the value will be *1*, otherwise *0*. Let's build a vector representing the e-mail with the *online pharmacy sale* content:

$$x = \begin{bmatrix} 0 \\ 0 \\ \dots \\ 1 \\ \dots \\ 1 \\ \dots \\ 1 \\ \dots \end{bmatrix} \begin{array}{l} a \\ aard-vark \\ \dots \\ online \\ \dots \\ pharmacy \\ \dots \\ sale \\ \dots \end{array}$$

The dictionary of words in this feature vector is called **vocabulary**, and the dimensions of the vector are the same as the size of the vocabulary. If the vocabulary size is 10,000, the possible values in this feature vector will be 210,000.

Our goal is to model the probability of x given y. To model $P(x|y)$, we will make a strong assumption, and that assumption is that x's are conditionally independent. This assumption is called the **Naïve Bayes** assumption, and the algorithm based on this assumption is called the **Naïve Bayes classifier**.

For example, for $y = 1$, which means spam, the probability of *online appearing* and *pharmacy appearing* are independent. This is a strong assumption that has nothing to do with reality but works out really well when it comes to getting good predictions.

Getting ready

We are going to use the same diabetes data we used in the previous recipe.

How to do it...

1. Start the Spark shell:

   ```
   $ spark-shell
   ```

2. Perform the required imports:

   ```
   scala> import org.apache.spark.ml.classification.NaiveBayes
   scala> import
   org.apache.spark.ml.evaluation.MulticlassClassificationEvaluator
   ```

3. Load the data into the DataFrame from S3:

   ```
   scala> val data =
   spark.read.format("libsvm").load("s3a://sparkcookbook/patientdata")
   ```

4. Split the data into `training` and `test` datasets:

   ```
   scala> val Array(trainingData, testData) =
   data.randomSplit(Array(0.7, 0.3))
   ```

5. Train the model with the `training` dataset:

   ```
   scala> val model = new NaiveBayes().fit(trainingData)
   ```

6. Do the prediction:

   ```
   scala> val predictions = model.transform(testData)
   ```

7. Evaluate the accuracy:

   ```
   scala> val evaluator = new MulticlassClassificationEvaluator()
   .setMetricName("accuracy")
   scala> val accuracy = evaluator.evaluate(predictions)
   ```

Here the accuracy is only 55 percent, which shows Naive Bayes is not the best algorithm for this dataset.

9
Unsupervised Learning

This chapter will cover how we can do unsupervised learning using MLlib, Spark's machine learning library.

This chapter is divided into the following recipes:

- Clustering using k-means
- Dimensionality reduction with principal component analysis
- Dimensionality reduction with singular value decomposition

Introduction

The following is Wikipedia's definition of unsupervised learning:

> *"In machine learning, the problem of unsupervised learning is that of trying to find hidden structure in unlabeled data."*

In contrast to supervised learning, where we have labeled data to train an algorithm, in unsupervised learning, we ask the algorithm to find a structure on its own. Let's take a look at the following sample dataset:

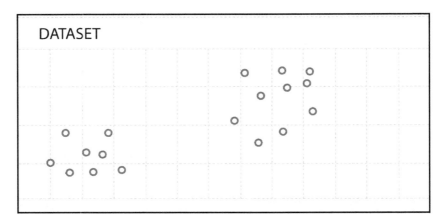

As you can see in the preceding graph, the data points are forming two clusters, as follows:

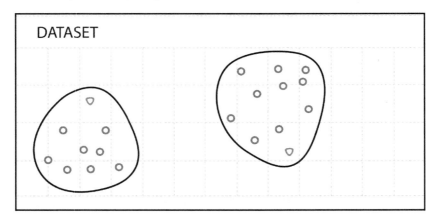

In fact, clustering is the most common type of unsupervised learning algorithm.

Clustering using k-means

Cluster analysis or clustering is the process of grouping data into multiple groups so that the data in one group would be similar to the data in other groups.

The following are a few examples where clustering is used:

- **Market segmentation**: Dividing the target market into multiple segments so that the needs of each segment can be served better
- **Social network analysis**: Finding a coherent group of people in the social network for ad targeting through a social networking site, such as Facebook
- **Data center computing clusters**: Putting a set of computers together to improve performance
- **Astronomical data analysis**: Understanding astronomical data and events, such as galaxy formations
- **Real estate**: Identifying neighborhoods based on similar features
- **Text analysis**: Dividing text documents, such as novels or essays, into genres

The k-means algorithm is best illustrated using imagery, so let's look at our sample figure again:

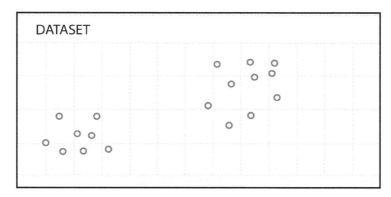

The first step in k-means is to randomly select two points called **cluster centroids**:

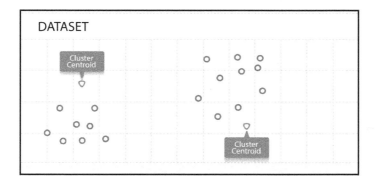

The k-means algorithm is an iterative algorithm and works in two steps:

1. **Cluster assignment step**: This algorithm will go through each data point, and it will be assigned the centroid it is nearer to and, in turn, the cluster it represents
2. **Move centroid step**: This algorithm will take each centroid and move it to the mean of the data points in the cluster

Let's see how our data looks after the cluster assignment:

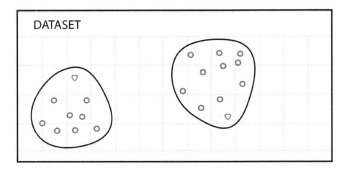

Now let's move the cluster centroids to the mean value of the data points in a cluster, as follows:

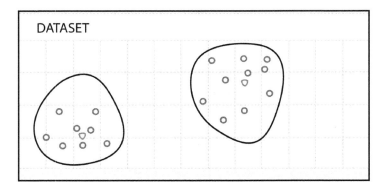

In this case, one iteration is enough; further iterations will not move the cluster centroids. For most real data, multiple iterations are required to move the centroid to the final position.

The k-means algorithm takes a number of clusters as input.

Getting ready

Let's use some different housing data from the City of Saratoga, CA. This time, we will look at the lot size and house price:

Lot size	House price (in $1,000)
12,839	**2,405**
10,000	2,200
8,040	1,400
13,104	1,800
10,000	2,351
3,049	795
38,768	2,725
16,250	2,150
43,026	2,724
44,431	2,675
40,000	2,930
1,260	870
15,000	2,210
10,032	1,145
12,420	2,419
69,696	2,750
12,600	2,035
10,240	1,150
876	665
8,125	1,430
11,792	1,920
1,512	1,230
1,276	975
67,518	2,400

Lot size	House price (in $1,000)
9,810	1,725
6,324	2,300
12,510	1,700
15,616	1,915
15476	2,278
13,390	2,497.5
1,158	725
2,000	870
2,614	730
13,433	2,050
12,500	3,330
15,750	1,120
13,996	4,100
10,450	1,655
7,500	1,550
12,125	2,100
14,500	2,100
10,000	1,175
10,019	2,047.5
48,787	3,998
53,579	2,688
10,788	2,251
11,865	1,906

Let's convert this data into a **comma-separated value** (**CSV**) file called `saratoga.csv` and draw it as a scatter plot:

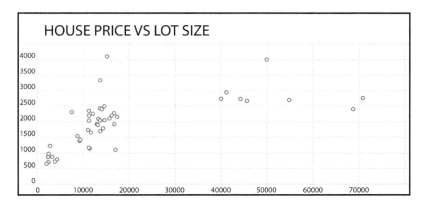

Finding the number of clusters is a tricky task. Here, we have the advantage of visual inspection, which is not available for data on hyperplanes (more than three dimensions). Let's roughly divide the data into four clusters as follows:

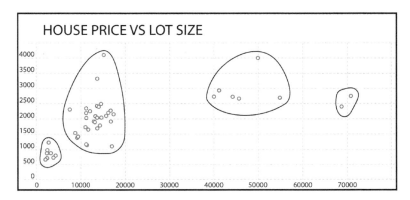

Run the k-means algorithm to do the same and see how close our results come.

How to do it...

1. Start the Spark shell:

```
$ spark-shell
```

2. Do the necessary imports:

```scala
scala> import org.apache.spark.ml.linalg.Vectors
scala> import org.apache.spark.ml.clustering.KMeans
```

3. Create a DataFrame with the features vector:

```scala
scala> val data = spark.createDataFrame(Seq(
   Vectors.dense(12839,2405),
   Vectors.dense(10000,2200),
   Vectors.dense(8040,1400),
   Vectors.dense(13104,1800),
   Vectors.dense(10000,2351),
   Vectors.dense(3049,795),
   Vectors.dense(38768,2725),
   Vectors.dense(16250,2150),
   Vectors.dense(43026,2724),
   Vectors.dense(44431,2675),
   Vectors.dense(40000,2930),
   Vectors.dense(1260,870),
   Vectors.dense(15000,2210),
   Vectors.dense(10032,1145),
   Vectors.dense(12420,2419),
   Vectors.dense(69696,2750),
   Vectors.dense(12600,2035),
   Vectors.dense(10240,1150),
   Vectors.dense(876,665),
   Vectors.dense(8125,1430),
   Vectors.dense(11792,1920),
   Vectors.dense(1512,1230),
   Vectors.dense(1276,975),
   Vectors.dense(67518,2400),
   Vectors.dense(9810,1725),
   Vectors.dense(6324,2300),
   Vectors.dense(12510,1700),
   Vectors.dense(15616,1915),
   Vectors.dense(15476,2278),
   Vectors.dense(13390,2497.5),
   Vectors.dense(1158,725),
   Vectors.dense(2000,870),
   Vectors.dense(2614,730),
   Vectors.dense(13433,2050),
   Vectors.dense(12500,3330),
   Vectors.dense(15750,1120),
   Vectors.dense(13996,4100),
   Vectors.dense(10450,1655),
   Vectors.dense(7500,1550),
   Vectors.dense(12125,2100),
```

```
        Vectors.dense(14500,2100),
        Vectors.dense(10000,1175),
        Vectors.dense(10019,2047.5),
        Vectors.dense(48787,3998),
        Vectors.dense(53579,2688),
        Vectors.dense(10788,2251),
        Vectors.dense(11865,1906)
    ).map(Tuple1.apply)).toDF("features")
```

4. Create a k-means estimator for the four clusters:

```
scala> val kmeans = new KMeans().setK(4).setSeed(1L)
```

5. Train the model:

```
scala> val model = kmeans.fit(data)
```

6. Now compare the cluster assignments by k-means versus the ones we have done individually. The k-means algorithm gives the cluster IDs, starting from *0*. Once you inspect the data, you will find that the mapping between the *A* and *D* cluster IDs we gave versus k-means is this: *A=>3, B=>0, C=>2, D=>1*.

7. Pick some data from different parts of the chart and predict which cluster it belongs to.

8. Look at the data for the 19th house, which has a lot size of 876 sq. ft. and is priced at $665K:

```
scala> val prediction = model.transform(spark.createDataFrame
(Seq(Vectors.dense(876,665)).map(Tuple1.apply)).toDF("features"))
scala> prediction.first.get(1)
resxx: Any = 3
```

9. Next, look at the data for the 36th house with a lot size of 15,750 sq. ft. and a price of $1.12 million:

```
scala> val prediction = model.transform(spark.createDataFrame
(Seq(Vectors.dense(15750,1120)).map(Tuple1.apply)).toDF("features"))
scala> prediction.first.get(1)
resxx: Any = 0
```

10. Now look at the data for the 7th house, which has a lot size of 38,768 sq. ft. and is priced at $2.725 million:

```
scala> val prediction = model.transform(spark.createDataFrame
(Seq(Vectors.dense(38768,2725)).map(Tuple1.apply)).toDF("features"))
       scala> prediction.first
resxx: Any = 2
```

11. Moving on, look at the data for the 16th house, which has a lot size of 69,696 sq. ft. and is priced at $2.75 million:

```
scala>  val prediction = model.transform(spark.createDataFrame
(Seq(Vectors.dense(69696,2750)).map(Tuple1.apply)).toDF("features"))
       scala> prediction.first
resxx: Any = 1
```

You can test prediction capability with more data. Let's do some neighborhood analysis to see what meaning these clusters carry. Most of the houses in cluster 3 are near downtown. Cluster 2 houses are on a hilly terrain.

In this example, we dealt with a very small set of features; common sense and visual inspection would also lead us to the same conclusions. The beauty of the k-means algorithm is that it does the clustering of the data with an unlimited number of features. It is a great tool to use when you have raw data and would like to know the patterns in that data.

Dimensionality reduction with principal component analysis

Dimensionality reduction is the process of reducing the number of dimensions or features. A lot of real data contains a very high number of features. It is not uncommon to have thousands of features. So we need to drill down to features that matter.

Dimensionality reduction serves several purposes, such as:

- Data compression
- Visualization

When the number of dimensions is reduced, it reduces the disk and memory footprint. Last but not least, it helps algorithms to run faster. It also helps reduce highly correlated dimensions to one.

Humans can only visualize three dimensions, but data has access to a much higher number of dimensions. Visualization can help find hidden patterns in a particular piece of data. Dimensionality reduction helps visualization by compacting multiple features into one.

The most popular algorithm for dimensionality reduction is **principal component analysis (PCA)**.

Let's look at the following dataset:

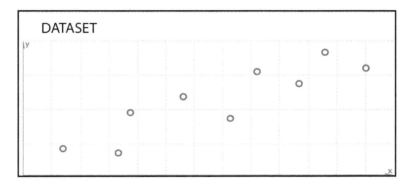

Let's say the goal is to divide this two-dimensional data into one dimension. The way to do this would be to find a line on which we can project this data. Let's find a line that is good for projecting this data on:

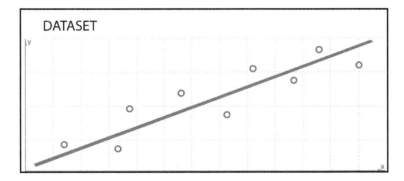

This is the line that has the shortest projected distance from the data points. Let's check this out further by dropping the shortest lines from each data point to this projected line:

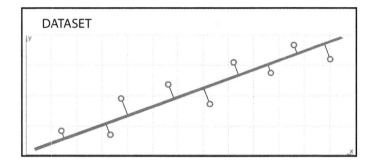

Another way to look at this is to find a line to project the data on so that the sum of the square distances of the data points from this line would be minimized. The gray line segments are also called **projection errors**.

Getting ready

Let's look at the three features of the housing data of the City of Saratoga, CA, that is, house size, lot size, and price. Using PCA, we will merge the house size and lot size features into one feature, namely z. Let's call this feature **z density of a house**.

It is worth noting that it is not always possible to give meaning to the new feature created. In this case, it is easy as we have only two features to combine and we can use common sense to combine the effect of the two. In a more practical case, you may have 1,000 features that you are trying to project to 100 features. It may not be possible to give real-life meaning to each one of those 100 features.

In this exercise, we will derive the housing density using PCA and then we will do linear regression to see how this density affects the house price.

There is a preprocessing stage before we delve into PCA: **feature scaling**. Feature scaling comes into the picture when two features have ranges that are at different scales. Here, house size varies in the range of 800 sq. ft. to 7,000 sq. ft., while the lot size varies between 800 sq. ft. to a few acres.

Why did we not have to do feature scaling before? The answer is that we really did not have to put features on a level-playing field. Gradient descent is another area where feature scaling is very useful.

There are different ways of doing feature scaling:

- Dividing a feature value with a maximum value that will put every feature in the *-1 ≤x ≤1* range
- Dividing a feature value with the range, that is, maximum value-minimum value
- Subtracting a feature value by its mean and then dividing it by the range
- Subtracting a feature value by its mean and then dividing it by the standard deviation

We are going to use the fourth choice to scale in the best way possible. The following is the data we are going to use for this recipe:

House size	Lot size	Scaled house size	Scaled lot size	House price (in $1,000)
2,524	**12,839**	**-0.025**	**-0.231**	**2,405**
2,937	10,000	0.323	-0.4	2,200
1,778	8,040	-0.654	-0.517	1,400
1,242	13,104	-1.105	-0.215	1,800
2,900	10,000	0.291	-0.4	2,351
1,218	3,049	-1.126	-0.814	795
2,722	38,768	0.142	1.312	2,725
2,553	16,250	-0.001	-0.028	2,150
3,681	43,026	0.949	1.566	2,724
3,032	44,431	0.403	1.649	2,675
3,437	40,000	0.744	1.385	2,930
1,680	1,260	-0.736	-0.92	870
2,260	15,000	-0.248	-0.103	2,210
1,660	10,032	-0.753	-0.398	1,145
3,251	12,420	0.587	-0.256	2,419
3,039	69,696	0.409	3.153	2,750
3,401	12,600	0.714	-0.245	2,035
1,620	10,240	-0.787	-0.386	1,150
876	876	-1.414	-0.943	665

House size	Lot size	Scaled house size	Scaled lot size	House price (in $1,000)
1,889	8,125	-0.56	-0.512	1,430
4,406	11,792	1.56	-0.294	1,920
1,885	1,512	-0.564	-0.905	1,230
1,276	1,276	-1.077	-0.92	975
3,053	67,518	0.42	3.023	2,400
2,323	9,810	-0.195	-0.412	1,725
3,139	6,324	0.493	-0.619	2,300
2,293	12,510	-0.22	-0.251	1,700
2,635	15,616	0.068	-0.066	1,915
2,298	15,476	-0.216	-0.074	2,278
2,656	13,390	0.086	-0.198	2,497.5
1,158	1,158	-1.176	-0.927	725
1,511	2,000	-0.879	-0.876	870
1,252	2,614	-1.097	-0.84	730
2,141	13,433	-0.348	-0.196	2,050
3,565	12,500	0.852	-0.251	3,330
1,368	15,750	-0.999	-0.058	1,120
5,726	13,996	2.672	-0.162	4,100
2,563	10,450	0.008	-0.373	1,655
1,551	7,500	-0.845	-0.549	1,550
1,993	12,125	-0.473	-0.274	2,100
2,555	14,500	0.001	-0.132	2,100
1,572	10,000	-0.827	-0.4	1,175
2,764	10,019	0.177	-0.399	2,047.5
7,168	48,787	3.887	1.909	3,998
4,392	53,579	1.548	2.194	2,688
3,096	10,788	0.457	-0.353	2,251

House size	Lot size	Scaled house size	Scaled lot size	House price (in $1,000)
2,003	11,865	-0.464	-0.289	1,906

Let's take the scaled house size and scaled house price data and save it as `scaledhousedata.csv`.

How to do it...

1. Load `scaledhousedata.csv` to HDFS:

   ```
   $ hdfs dfs -put scaledhousedata.csv scaledhousedata.csv
   ```

2. Start the Spark shell:

   ```
   $ spark-shell
   ```

3. Import the statistics and related classes:

   ```
   scala> import org.apache.spark.mllib.linalg.Vectors
   scala> import org.apache.spark.mllib.linalg.distributed.RowMatrix
   ```

4. Load `scaledhousedata.csv` as an RDD:

   ```
   scala> val data = sc.textFile("scaledhousedata.csv")
   ```

5. For your convenience, data has already been loaded into S3, and you can load it using the following command:

   ```
   scala> val data =
   sc.textFile("s3a://sparkcookbook/saratoga/scaledhousedata.csv")
   ```

6. Transform the data into an RDD of dense vectors:

   ```
   scala> val parsedData = data.map( line =>
   Vectors.dense(line.split(',').map(_.toDouble)))
   ```

7. Create `RowMatrix` from `parsedData`:

   ```
   scala> val mat = new RowMatrix(parsedData)
   ```

8. Compute one principal component:

   ```
   scala> val pc= mat.computePrincipalComponents(1)
   ```

9. Project the rows to the linear space spanned by the principal component:

```scala
scala> val projected = mat.multiply(pc)
```

10. Convert the projected RowMatrix object back to the RDD:

```scala
scala> val projectedRDD = projected.rows
```

11. Save projectedRDD to HDFS:

```scala
scala> projectedRDD.saveAsTextFile("phdata")
```

Now we will use this projected feature, which we have decided to call housing density, and plot it against the house price and see whether any new pattern emerges:

1. Download the HDFS directory phdata to the local directory phdata:

```scala
scala> hdfs dfs -get phdata phdata
```

2. Trim the start and end brackets in the data and load it into MS Excel, next to the house price. The following is the plot of the house price versus the housing density:

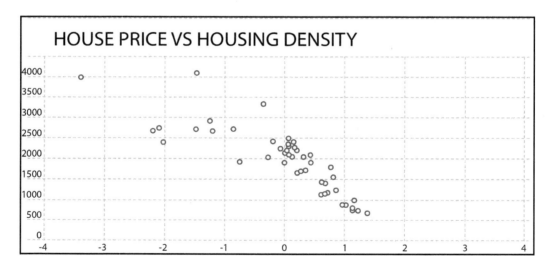

Let's draw some patterns of this data as follows:

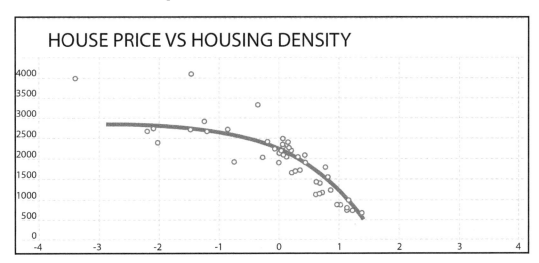

What patterns do we see here? For moving from very high-density to low-density housing, people are ready to pay a heavy premium. As the housing density reduces, the premium flattens out. For example, people will pay a heavy premium to move from condominiums and town homes to a single-family home, but the premium for a single-family home with a three-acre lot size is not going to be much different from a single-family house with a two-acre lot size in a comparable built-up area.

Dimensionality reduction with singular value decomposition

Often, the original dimensions do not represent data in the best way possible. As we saw in PCA, you can, sometimes, project data to fewer dimensions and still retain most of the useful information.

Sometimes, the best approach is to align dimensions along the features that exhibit the most number of variations. This approach helps eliminate dimensions that are not representative of the data.

Let's look at the following figure again, which shows the best-fitting line on two dimensions:

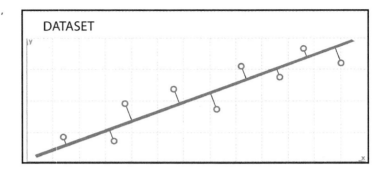

The projection line shows the best approximation of the original data with one dimension. If we take the points where the gray line is intersecting with the black line and isolating it, we will have a reduced representation of the original data with as much variation retained as possible, as shown in the following figure:

Let's draw a line perpendicular to the first projection line, as shown in the following figure:

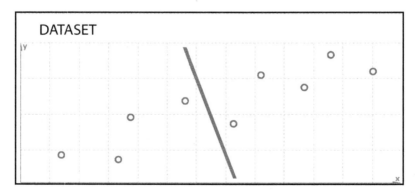

This line captures as much variation as possible along the second dimension of the original dataset. It does a bad job at approximating the original data as this dimension exhibits less variation to start with. It is possible to use these projection lines to generate a set of uncorrelated data points that will show subgroupings in the original data, not visible at first glance.

This is the basic idea behind **Singular Value Decomposition** (**SVD**). Take a high dimension, a highly variable set of data points, and reduce it to a lower dimensional space that exposes the structure of the original data more clearly and orders it from having the most amount of variation to the least. What makes SVD very useful, especially for NLP application, is that you can simply ignore variation below a certain threshold to massively reduce the original data, making sure that the original relationship interests are retained.

Let's get into theory now. SVD is based on a theorem of linear algebra that a rectangular matrix A can be broken down into a product of three matrices: an orthogonal matrix U, a diagonal matrix S, and the transpose of an orthogonal matrix V. We can show this as follows:

$$A = USV^T$$

U and V are orthogonal matrices:

$$U^T U = 1$$

$$V^T V = 1$$

The columns of U are orthonormal eigenvectors of AA^T, and the columns of V are orthonormal eigenvectors of $A^T A$. S is a diagonal matrix containing the square roots of eigenvalues from U or V in descending order.

Getting ready

Let's look at an example of a term-document matrix. We are going to look at two news items about the US presidential elections.

The following are the links to the two documents:

- **Fox:** http://www.foxnews.com/politics/2015/03/08/top-2016-gop-presiden tial-hopefuls-return-to-iowa-to-hone-message-including/
- **Npr:** http://www.npr.org/blogs/itsallpolitics/2015/03/09/391704815/in-iowa-2 016-has-begun-at-least-for-the-republican-party

Let's build the presidential candidate matrix out of these two news items:

$$npr \quad fox$$

$$
\begin{array}{r}
ChrisChristie \\
JebBush \\
MikeHuckabee \\
GeorgePataki \\
RickSantorum \\
LindseyGraham \\
TedCruz \\
ScottWalker \\
RickScott \\
HillaryClinton \\
MarkRubio \\
RickPerry
\end{array}
\begin{bmatrix}
1 & 2 \\
2 & 3 \\
1 & 4 \\
1 & 0 \\
1 & 0 \\
1 & 3 \\
1 & 2 \\
1 & 0 \\
1 & 2 \\
0 & 3 \\
0 & 1 \\
0 & 2
\end{bmatrix}
$$

Let's put this matrix in a CSV file and then put it in HDFS. We will apply SVD to this matrix and analyze the results.

How to do it...

1. Load `pres.csv` to HDFS:

   ```
   $ hdfs dfs -put pres.csv
   ```

2. Start the Spark shell:

   ```
   $ spark-shell
   ```

3. Import the statistics and related classes:

   ```
   scala> import org.apache.spark.mllib.linalg.Vectors
   scala> import org.apache.spark.mllib.linalg.distributed.RowMatrix
   ```

4. Load `pres.csv` as an RDD:

   ```
   scala> val data = sc.textFile("pres.csv")
   ```

5. Transform data into an RDD of dense vectors:

```scala
scala> val parsedData = data.map( line =>
Vectors.dense(line.split(',').map(_.toDouble)))
```

6. Create `RowMatrix` from `parsedData`:

```scala
scala> val mat = new RowMatrix(parsedData)
```

7. Compute `svd`:

```scala
scala> val svd = mat.computeSVD(2,true)
```

8. Calculate the `U` factor (eigenvector):

```scala
scala> val U = svd.U
```

9. Calculate the matrix of singular values (eigenvalues):

```scala
scala> val s = svd.s
```

10. Calculate the `V` factor (eigenvector):

```scala
scala> val s = svd.s
```

If you look at `s`, you will realize that it gave a much higher score to the Npr article than the Fox article.

10
Recommendations Using Collaborative Filtering

In this chapter, we will cover the following recipes:

- Collaborative filtering using explicit feedback
- Collaborative filtering using implicit feedback

Introduction

The following is Wikipedia's definition of recommender systems:

> *"Recommender systems are a subclass of information filtering system that seeks to predict the rating or preference that user would give to an item."*

Recommender systems have gained immense popularity in recent years. Amazon uses them to recommend books, Netflix for movies, and Google News to recommend news stories. As the proof is in the pudding, here are some examples of the impact recommendations can have (source: Celma, Lamere, 2008):

- Two-thirds of the movies watched on Netflix are recommended
- 38 % of the news clicks on Google News are recommended
- 35 % of the sales at Amazon sales are the result of recommendations

As we saw in the previous chapters, features and feature selection play a major role in the efficacy of machine learning algorithms. Recommender engine algorithms discover these features, called **latent features**, automatically. In short, there are latent features responsible for a user to like one movie and dislike another. If another user has corresponding latent features, there is a good chance that this person will also have a similar taste for movies.

To understand this better, let's look at some sample movie ratings:

Movie	Rich	Bob	Peter	Chris
Titanic	5	3	5	?
GoldenEye	3	2	1	5
Toy Story	1	?	2	2
Disclosure	4	4	?	4
Ace Ventura	4	?	4	?

Our goal is to predict the missing entries shown with the **?** symbol. Let's see if we can find some features associated with the movies. At first, you will look at the genres, as shown here:

Movie	Genre
Titanic	Action and Romance
GoldenEye	Action, Adventure, and Thriller
Toy Story	Animation, Children's, and Comedy
Disclosure	Drama and Thriller
Ace Ventura	Comedy

Now, each movie can be rated for each genre from 0 to 1. For example, GoldenEye is not primarily a romance, so it may have 0.1 rating for romance, but a 0.98 rating for action. Therefore, each movie can be represented as a **feature vector**.

In this chapter, we are going to use the MovieLens dataset from grouplens.org/datasets/movielens/ for F. Maxwell Harper and Joseph A. Konstan, 2015. Go to *The MovieLens Dataset: History and Context, ACM Transactions on Interactive Intelligent Systems (TiiS)* 5, 4, Article 19 (December 2015), 19 pages. DOI http://dx.doi.org/10.1145/2827872.

The InfoObjects big data sandbox comes loaded with 1 million movie ratings. In this recipe, we are using 20 million ratings, which have been loaded on S3 for your convenience. Since it will require heavy-duty compute, we recommend using either Databricks Cloud or EMR. Feel free to use Sandbox if you have a machine with server-level configuration.

We are going to use two files from this dataset:

- `ratings.csv`: This has a comma-separated list of movie ratings in the following format:

  ```
  user id , movie id , rating , epoch time
  ```

  Since we are not going to need the timestamp, we are going to filter it out from the data in our recipe

- `movies.csv`: This has a comma-separated list of movies in the following format:

  ```
  movie id | movie title | genre
  ```

This chapter will cover how we can make recommendations using Spark ML.

Collaborative filtering using explicit feedback

Collaborative filtering is the most commonly used technique for recommender systems. It has an interesting property—it learns the features on its own. So, in the case of movie ratings, we do not need to provide actual human feedback on whether the movie is romantic or action.

As we saw, in the preceding section, movies have some latent features, such as genre, in the same way, users have some latent features, such as age, gender, and more. Collaborative filtering does not need them; it figures out latent features on its own.

We are going to use an algorithm called **alternating least squares** (ALS) in this example. This algorithm explains the association between a movie and a user based on a small number of latent features. It uses three training parameters: `rank`, `number of iterations`, and `lambda` (explained later in the chapter). The best way to figure out the optimum values of these three parameters is to try different values and see which value has the smallest amount of **root mean square error** (RMSE). This error is like a standard deviation, but it is based on model results rather than actual data.

Getting ready

We are going to use the `moviedata` folder in S3:

```
s3a://sparkcookbook/moviedata
```

We are going to add some personalized ratings to this database so that we can test the accuracy of the recommendations.

You can look at `movie.ratings` to pick some movies and rate them. Feel free to choose the movies you would like to rate and provide your own ratings. The following are some movies I chose, alongside my ratings:

Movie ID	Movie name	Rating (1-5)
1721	Titanic	5
10	GoldenEye	3
1	Toy Story	1
225	Disclosure	4
344	Ace Ventura: Pet Detective	4
480	Jurassic Park	5
589	Terminator 2	5
780	Independence Day	4
1049	The Ghost and the Darkness	4

The highest user ID is 138493, so we are going to add the new user as 138494 to associate with these ratings further down in the recipe.

How to do it...

1. Start Spark shell or Scala shell in Databricks Cloud:

   ```
   $ spark-shell
   ```

2. Import the **Alternating Least Squares** (**ALS**) and `rating` classes:

   ```
   scala> import org.apache.spark.ml.recommendation.ALS
   scala> import
     org.apache.spark.ml.evaluation.RegressionEvaluator
   ```

3. Create a `Rating` case class:

```scala
scala> case class Rating(userId: Int, movieId: Int, rating: Double,
timestamp: Long)
```

4. Load the `ratings` data as a `Rating` dataset:

```scala
scala> val ratings =
spark.read.option("header","true").option("inferschema","true").csv("s3a://
sparkcookbook/moviedata/ratings.csv").as[Rating].cache
```

5. Split into `test` and `training` dataset:

```scala
scala> val Array(training, test) = ratings.randomSplit(Array(0.7,
0.3))
```

6. Initialize `ALS()` function:

```scala
scala> val als = new
ALS().setMaxIter(30).setRegParam(.065).setUserCol("userId").setItemCol("mov
ieId")
 .setRatingCol("rating")
```

7. Do model training:

```scala
scala> val model = als.fit(training)
```

8. Calculate predictions on the `test` dataset:

```scala
scala> val predictions = model.transform(test).na.drop
```

`df.na.drop` drops any rows containing null values. For the curious, this method is in the
class `org.apache.spark.sql.DataFrameNaFunctions`. Go to GitHub and take a dive into the code.

9. Initialize the `evaluator`:

```scala
scala> val evaluator = new RegressionEvaluator()
.setMetricName("rmse")
.setLabelCol("rating")
.setPredictionCol("prediction")
```

10. Calculate root-mean-square error (`rmse`):

```scala
scala> val rmse = evaluator.evaluate(predictions)
```

11. Print `rmse`:

```scala
scala> println(s"Root-mean-square error = $rmse")
```
Root-mean-square error = 0.7914419472440173

 Root-mean-square error is mainly how much variance the predictions have from labels. The value is measured relative to the range outcome variable and has the same units as the outcome variable (in this case, ratings 0-5).

Adding my recommendations and then testing predictions

It is good to see the evaluation metric, but to make it more fun, let's add my recommendations as created in the preceding section and then make predictions on some interesting movies:

1. Let's redo training by adding my recommendations to the training data:

```scala
val myrecs = spark.createDataFrame(Seq(
    (138494,1721,5,1489789319),
    (138494,10,3,1489789319),
    (138494,1,1,1489789319),
    (138494,225,4,1489789319),
    (138494,344,4,1489789319),
    (138494,480,5,1489789319),
    (138494,589,5,1489789319),
    (138494,780,4,1489789319),
    (138494,1049,4,1489789319)
)).toDF("userId","movieId","rating","timestamp").as[Rating]
```

2. Create a new training set by adding `myrecs` to the training set:

```scala
scala> val trainingWithMyRecs = training.union(myrecs)
```

3. Train the model again:

```scala
scala> val model = als.fit(trainingWithMyRecs)
```

4. Let's start with creating a dataset for the original Terminator with movie ID 1240:

```scala
scala> val terminator = spark.createDataFrame(Seq(
(138494,1240) )).toDF("userId","movieId")
```

5. Let's run the prediction:

```scala
scala> val p = model.transform(terminator)
```

6. Let's see the result:

```
scala> p.show
+------+-------+----------+
|userId|movieId|prediction|
+------+-------+----------+
|138494| 1240  |  4.091806|
+------+-------+----------+
```

Since I rated Terminator 2 as 5, this is a reasonable prediction.

7. Let's try Ghost with movie ID 587:

```scala
scala> val ghost = spark.createDataFrame(Seq(   (138494,587)
)).toDF("userId","movieId")
scala> val p = model.transform(ghost)
scala> p.show
+------+-------+----------+
|userId|movieId|prediction|
+------+-------+----------+
|138494|  587|  3.8229413|
+------+-------+----------+
```

Good guess.

Let's try *The Ghost and the Darkness*, the movie I already rated, with the ID 1049:

```scala
scala> val gnd = spark.createDataFrame(Seq(
  (138494,1049)
)).toDF("userId","movieId")
scala> val p = model.transform(gnd)
scala> p.show
+------+-------+----------+
|userId|movieId|prediction|
+------+-------+----------+
|138494| 1049|  3.7397728|
+------+-------+----------+
```

Very close prediction, knowing that I rated the movie 4.

There's more...

There are two types of recommender algorithms:

- Content-based filtering
- Collaborative filtering

In content-based filtering, each user is assumed to operate independently. Recommendations to the user are based on keywords, which represent an item.

In collaborative filtering, an item is associated with the ratings users have provided about this item collectively. The basic premise of collaborative filtering is this, *if two users like a subset of items, there is a good chance they will like the rest of the items in the set too.*

The most interesting characteristic of collaborative filtering is that it is *neutral* to the type of item being rated.

Collaborative filtering using implicit feedback

Sometimes, the feedback available is not in the form of ratings but in the form of audio tracks played, movies watched, and so on. This data, at first glance, may not look as good as explicit ratings by users, but this is much more exhaustive.

How to do it...

We are going to use the million song data from `http://www.kaggle.com/c/msdchallenge/data`. You need to download three files:

- `kaggle_visible_evaluation_triplets`
- `kaggle_users.txt`
- `kaggle_songs.txt`

We still need to do some more preprocessing. ALS in MLlib takes both user and product IDs as integers. The `Kaggle_songs.txt` file has song IDs and a sequence number next to it. The `Kaggle_users.txt` file does not have a sequence number. Our goal is to replace the `userid` and `songid` in the `triplets` data with the corresponding integer sequence numbers. To do this, follow these steps:

1. Start Spark shell or Databricks Cloud (preferred):

   ```
   $ spark-shell
   ```

2. Do the necessary imports:

   ```
   import org.apache.spark.ml.recommendation.ALS
   import org.apache.spark.sql.functions._
   import org.apache.spark.ml.evaluation.RegressionEvaluator
   ```

3. Initialize the `ALS()` function:

   ```
   val als = new ALS()
   .setImplicitPrefs(true)
   .setUserCol("userId")
   .setItemCol("songId")
   .setRatingCol("plays")
   ```

4. Load the `kaggle_songs.txt` data as a DataFrame:

   ```
   scala> val songs = spark.read.option("delimiter","
   ").option("inferschema","true").csv("s3a://sparkcookbook/songdata/kaggle_so
   ngs.txt").toDF("song","songId")
   ```

5. Load as temporary view:

   ```
   scala> songs.createOrReplaceTempView("songs")
   ```

6. Load the user data as a DataFrame:

   ```
   scala> val users =
   spark.read.textFile("s3a://sparkcookbook/songdata/kaggle_users.txt").toDF("
   user").withColumn("userId",monotonically_increasing_id)
   ```

7. Cast `userId` as `integer` (by default, it gets loaded as `long`, but maximum value fits well in the integer range, ALS expects `UserId` and `ItemId` to be an `integer`):

   ```
   scala> val u =
   users.withColumn("userId",users.col("userId").cast("integer"))
   ```

8. Create temporary view:

```scala
scala> u.createOrReplaceTempView("users")
```

9. Load the `triplets` (user, song, plays) data as a dataset:

```scala
scala> val triplets =
spark.read.option("delimiter","t").option("inferschema","true").csv("s3a://
sparkcookbook/songdata/kaggle_visible_evaluation_triplets.txt").toDF("user"
,"song","plays")
```

10. Cast `plays` to `double`:

```scala
scala> val t =
triplets.withColumn("plays",triplets.col("plays").cast("double"))
```

11. Load as temporary view:

```scala
scala> t.createOrReplaceTempView("plays")
```

12. Create DataFrame with `userId`, `songId`, `plays` tuple:

```scala
scala> val plays = spark.sql("select userId,songId,plays from plays
p join users u on p.user = u.user join songs s on p.song = s.song")
```

13. Create `training`, `test` split:

```scala
scala> val Array(training, test) = plays.randomSplit(Array(0.7,
0.3))
```

14. Train the model:

```scala
scala> val model = als.fit(training)
```

15. Do predictions on the `test` dataset:

```scala
scala> val predictions = model.transform(test).na.drop
```

16. Load `evaluator`:

```scala
scala> val evaluator = new RegressionEvaluator()
.setMetricName("mae")
.setLabelCol("plays")
.setPredictionCol("prediction")
```

17. Evaluate results:

```scala
scala> val rmse = evaluator.evaluate(predictions)
```

11
Graph Processing Using GraphX and GraphFrames

This chapter will cover how we can do graph processing using GraphX, Spark's graph processing library.

The chapter is divided into the following recipes:

- Fundamental operations on graphs
- Using PageRank
- Finding connected components
- Performing neighborhood aggregation
- Understanding GraphFrames

Introduction

Graph analysis is much more commonplace in our life than we think. To take the most common example, when we ask a **Global Positioning System** (**GPS**) to find the shortest route to a destination, it uses a graph-processing algorithm.

Let's start by understanding graphs. A graph is a representation of a set of vertices, where some pairs of vertices are connected by edges. When these edges move from one direction to another, it's called a **directed graph** or **digraph**.

GraphX is the Spark API for graph processing. It provides a wrapper around an RDD called a **resilient distributed property graph**. The property graph is a directed multigraph, with properties attached to each vertex and edge.

There are two types of graphs—directed graphs (digraphs) and regular graphs. Directed graphs have edges that run in one direction; for example, from vertex *A* to vertex *B*. A Twitter follower is a good example of a digraph. If John is David's Twitter follower, it does not mean that David is John's follower. On the other hand, Facebook is a good example of a regular graph. If John is David's Facebook friend, David is also John's Facebook friend.

A multigraph is a graph that is allowed to have multiple edges (also called **parallel edges**). Since every edge in GraphX has properties, each edge has its own identity.

Traditionally, for distributed graph processing, there have been two types of systems:

- Data parallel
- Graph parallel

GraphX aims to combine the two together in one system. The GraphX API enables users to view the data both as graphs and as collections (RDDs), without data movement.

Fundamental operations on graphs

In this recipe, we will learn how to create graphs and do basic operations on them.

Getting ready

As a starting example, we will have three vertices, each representing the city center of three cities in California—Santa Clara, Fremont, and San Francisco. The following is a roughly drawn out geographic position of the three cities (not to scale):

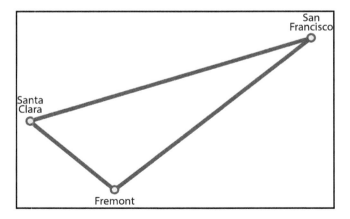

The following is the distance between these cities:

Source	Destination	Distance (miles)
Santa Clara, CA	Fremont, CA	20
Fremont, CA	San Francisco, CA	44
San Francisco, CA	Santa Clara, CA	53

How to do it...

1. Import the `graphx` related classes:

```scala
scala> import org.apache.spark.graphx._
scala> import org.apache.spark.rdd.RDD
```

2. Load the vertex data in an array:

```scala
scala> val vertices = Array((1L, ("Santa Clara","CA")),(2L,
    ("Fremont","CA")),(3L, ("San Francisco","CA")))
```

3. Load the array of vertices into the RDD of vertices:

```scala
scala> val vrdd = sc.parallelize(vertices)
```

4. Load the edge data in an array:

```scala
scala> val edges = Array(Edge(1L,2L,20),Edge(2L,3L,44)
    ,Edge(3L,1L,53))
```

5. Load the data into the RDD of `edges`:

```scala
scala> val erdd = sc.parallelize(edges)
```

6. Create the graph:

```scala
scala> val graph = Graph(vrdd,erdd)
```

7. Print all the vertices of the graph:

```scala
scala> graph.vertices.collect.foreach(println)
```

8. Print all the edges of the graph:

```scala
scala> graph.edges.collect.foreach(println)
```

9. Print the edge triplets; a triplet is created by adding source and destination attributes to an edge:

```scala
scala> graph.triplets.collect.foreach(println)
```

10. An in-degree of a graph is the number of inward-directed edges it has. Print the in-degree of each vertex (as `VertexRDD[Int]`):

```scala
scala> graph.inDegrees.foreach(println)
```

Using PageRank

PageRank measures the importance of each vertex in a graph. PageRank was started by Google's founders, who used the theory that the most important pages on the Internet are the pages with the most links leading to them. PageRank also looks at the importance of a page leading to the target page. So, if a given web page has incoming links from higher rank pages, it will be ranked higher.

Getting ready

We are going to use Wikipedia's page link data to calculate the page rank. Wikipedia publishes its data in the form of a database dump. We are going to use link data from, which has the data in two files:

- `links-simple-sorted.txt`
- `titles-sorted.txt`

 I have put both of them on Amazon S3 at `s3a://com.infoobjects.wiki/links` and `s3a://com.infoobjects.wiki/nodes`. Since the data size is larger, it is recommended that you run it on either Databricks Cloud or EMR.

How to do it...

1. Import the `graphx` related classes:

```scala
scala> import org.apache.spark.graphx._
```

2. Load the edges from Amazon S3:

```scala
scala> val edgesFile = sc.textFile(
  "s3a://com.infoobjects.wiki/links",20)
```

The links file has links in the *sourcelink: link1 link2 ...* format.

3. Flatten and convert `edgesFile` into an RDD of `link1, link2` format, and then convert it into an RDD of `Edge` objects:

```scala
scala> val edges = edgesFile.flatMap { line =>
val links = line.split("\\W+")
val from = links(0)
  val to = links.tail
for ( link <- to) yield (from,link)
 }.map( e => Edge(e._1.toLong,e._2.toLong,1))
```

Use the paste to copy multi-line code, and then execute using *Ctrl+D*.

4. Load the edges from Amazon S3:

```scala
scala> val verticesFile = sc.textFile
  ("s3a://com.infoobjects.wiki/nodes",20)
```

5. Provide an index to the vertices, and then swap it to make it in the `(index, title)` format:

```scala
scala> val vertices = verticesFile.zipWithIndex.map(_.swap)
```

6. Create the graph object:

```scala
scala> val graph = Graph(vertices,edges)
```

7. Run `pageRank` function, and get the vertices:

```scala
scala> val ranks = graph.pageRank(0.001).vertices
```

8. As ranks are in the (vertex ID, pagerank) format, swap it to make it in the (pagerank, vertex ID) format:

```scala
scala> val swappedRanks = ranks.map(_.swap)
```

9. Sort to get the highest ranked pages first:

```scala
scala> val sortedRanks = swappedRanks.sortByKey(false)
```

10. Get the highest ranked page:

```scala
scala> val highest = sortedRanks.first
```

11. The preceding command gives the vertex ID, which you still have to look up to see the actual title with the rank. Let's do a join:

```scala
scala> val join = sortedRanks.join(vertices)
```

12. Sort the joined RDD again after converting from the (vertex ID, (page rank, title)) format to the (page rank, (vertex ID, title)) format:

```scala
scala> val result = join.map ( v => (v._2._1,
    (v._1,v._2._2))).sortByKey(false)
```

13. Print the top five ranked pages:

```scala
scala> result.take(5).collect.foreach(println)
```

14. Here's what the output should be:

```
(12406.054646736622,
(5302153,United_States'_Country_Reports_on_Human_Rights_Practices))
(7925.094429748747,(84707,2007,_Canada_budget))
(7635.6564216408515,(88822,2008,_Madrid_plane_crash))
(7041.479913258444,(1921890,Geographic_coordinates))
(5675.169862343964,(5300058,United_Kingdom's))
```

Finding connected components

A connected component is a **subgraph** (a graph whose vertices are a subset of the vertex set of the original graph and whose edges are a subset of the edge set of the original graph) in which any two vertices are connected to each other by an edge or a series of edges.

An easy way to understand it would be by taking a look at the road network graph of *Hawaii*. This state has numerous islands, which are not connected by roads. Within each island, most roads will be connected to each other. The goal of finding the connected components is to find these clusters.

The connected components algorithm labels each connected component of the graph with the ID of its lowest-numbered vertex.

Getting ready

We will build a small graph here for the clusters we know and use connected components to segregate them. Let's look at the following data:

Follower	Followee
John	Pat
Pat	Dave
Gary	Chris
Chris	Bill

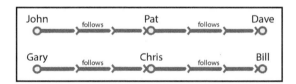

The preceding data is a simple one, with six vertices and two clusters. Let's put this data in the form of two files: nodes.csv and edges.csv.

The following is the content of `nodes.csv`:

```
1,John
2,Pat
3,Dave
4,Gary
5,Chris
6,Bill
```

The following is the content of `edges.csv`:

```
1,2,follows
2,3,follows
4,5,follows
5,6,follows
```

We should expect a connected component algorithm to identify two clusters, the first one is identified by `(1,John)` and the second by `(4,Gary)`.

You can load the files to HDFS using the following commands:

```
$ hdfs dfs -mkdir data/cc
$ hdfs dfs -put nodes.csv data/cc/nodes.csv
$ hdfs dfs -put edges.csv data/cc/edges.csv
```

How to do it...

1. Load the `spark-shell`:

   ```
   $ spark-shell
   ```

2. Import the `graphx` related classes:

   ```
   scala> import org.apache.spark.graphx._
   ```

3. Load the edges from `hdfs`:

   ```
   scala> val edgesFile = sc.textFile(
       "hdfs://localhost:9000/user/hduser/data/cc/edges.csv")
   ```

4. Convert the `edgesFile` RDD into the RDD of edges:

   ```
   scala> val edges = edgesFile.map(_.split(",")).map(e =>
       Edge(e(0).toLong,e(1).toLong,e(2)))
   ```

5. Load the vertices from HDFS:

```
scala> val verticesFile = sc.textFile(
  "hdfs://localhost:9000/user/hduser/data/cc/nodes.csv")
```

6. Map the vertices:

```
scala> val vertices = verticesFile.map(_.split(",")).map( e =>
  (e(0).toLong, e(1)))
```

7. Create the graph object:

```
scala> val graph = Graph(vertices, edges)
```

8. Calculate the connected components using graph.connectedComponents:

```
scala> val cc = graph.connectedComponents
```

9. Find the vertices for the connected components (which is a subgraph):

```
scala> val ccVertices = cc.vertices
```

10. Print the ccVertices:

```
scala> ccVertices.collect.foreach(println)
(4,4)
(6,4)
(2,1)
(1,1)
(3,1)
(5,4)
```

As you can see in the output, vertices *1*, *2*, and *3* are pointing to *1*, while *4*, *5*, and *6* are pointing to *4*. Both of these are the lowest-indexed vertices in their respective clusters.

Performing neighborhood aggregation

GraphX does most of the computation by isolating each vertex and its neighbors. It makes it easier to process the massive graph data on distributed systems. This makes the neighborhood operations very important. GraphX has a mechanism to do it at each neighborhood level in the form of the aggregateMessages method. It does it in two steps:

1. In the first step (the first function of the method), messages are sent to the destination vertex or source vertex (similar to the Map function in MapReduce).

2. In the second step (the second function of the method), aggregation is done on these messages (similar to the `Reduce` function in MapReduce).

Getting ready

Let's build a small dataset of the followers:

Follower	Followee
John	Barack
Pat	Barack
Gary	Barack
Chris	Mitt
Rob	Mitt

Our goal is to find out how many followers each node has. Let's load this data in the form of two files: `nodes.csv` and `edges.csv`.

The following is the content of `nodes.csv`:

```
1,Barack
2,John
3,Pat
4,Gary
5,Mitt
6,Chris
7,Rob
```

The following is the content of `edges.csv`:

```
2,1,follows
3,1,follows
4,1,follows
6,5,follows
7,5,follows
```

You can load the files to `hdfs` using the following commands:

```
$ hdfs dfs -mkdir data/na
$ hdfs dfs -put nodes.csv data/na/nodes.csv
$ hdfs dfs -put edges.csv data/na/edges.csv
```

How to do it...

1. Load the `spark-shell`:

   ```
   $ spark-shell
   ```

2. Import the `graphx` related classes:

   ```
   scala> import org.apache.spark.graphx._
   ```

3. Load the edges from HDFS:

   ```
   scala> val edgesFile = sc.textFile(
     "hdfs://localhost:9000/user/hduser/data/na/edges.csv")
   ```

4. Convert the edges into the RDD of edges:

   ```
   scala> val edges = edgesFile.map(_.split(",")).map(e =>
     Edge(e(0).toLong,e(1).toLong,e(2)))
   ```

5. Load the vertices from HDFS:

   ```
   scala> val verticesFile = sc.textFile(
     "hdfs://localhost:9000/user/hduser/data/cc/nodes.csv")
   ```

6. Map the vertices:

   ```
   scala> val vertices = verticesFile.map(_.split(",")).map( e =>
     (e(0).toLong,e(1)))
   ```

7. Create the `graph` object:

   ```
   scala> val graph = Graph(vertices,edges)
   ```

8. Do the neighborhood aggregation by sending messages to the followees with the number of followers from each follower, that is, *1*, and then adding the number of followers:

   ```
   scala> val followerCount = graph.aggregateMessages[(Int)]( t =>
     t.sendToDst(1), (a, b) => (a+b))
   ```

9. Print `followerCount` in the form of `(followee, number of followers)`:

   ```
   scala> followerCount.collect.foreach(println)
   ```

10. You should get an output similar to the following:

```
(1,3)
(5,2)
```

Understanding GraphFrames

As everything in the Spark world has moved to DataFrames, it is natural to wonder how GraphX is still RDD based. This is where GraphFrames comes into the picture. GraphFrames is still not directly included in the Spark library and is being developed separately as a Spark package. It is just a matter of time before it is considered stable enough to be included in the main API.

In this recipe, we will understand GraphFrames. The GraphFrames has two primary DataFrames:

- The vertices DataFrame, which needs to have a mandatory column called `id`
    - The edges DataFrame, which needs to have two mandatory columns, `src` and `dst`

Besides these requirements, both the `vertices` and `edges` DataFrames can have any arbitrary number and type of columns to represent attributes.

How to do it...

To get started with the recipe, we first need to perform the following steps:

1. Start `spark-shell` with the `graphframes` package:

```
$ spark-shell --packages graphframes:graphframes:0.2.0-
   spark2.0-s_2.11
```

 If you are getting an error downloading `slf4j`, please use following command to download it explicitly:
```
$ mvn org.apache.maven.plugins:maven-dependency-
plugin:2.4:get -DartifactId=slf4j-api -DgroupId=org.slf4j
-Dversion=1.7.7
```

2. Do the necessary imports:

```
scala> import org.graphframes._
```

3. Load the vertex DataFrame:

```scala
scala> val vertices = spark.sqlContext.createDataFrame
  (List(("sc","Santa Clara","CA"),("fr","Fremont","CA"),
    ("sf","San Francisco","CA"))).toDF("id","city","state")
```

4. Load the edge DataFrame:

```scala
scala> val edges = spark.sqlContext.createDataFrame
  (List(("sc","fr",20),("fr","sf",44),
    ("sf","sc",53))).toDF("src","dst","distance")
```

5. Create a GraphFrame:

```scala
scala> val g = GraphFrame(vertices, edges)
```

6. Show all vertices:

```scala
scala> g.vertices.show
```

7. Show all edges:

```scala
scala> g.edges.show
```

8. Get in-degrees of each vertex:

```scala
scala> g.inDegrees.show
```

Now that we have played with the toy dataset, let's do some exercise on a real dataset. We are going to use the California road network dataset as part of the **Stanford Network Analysis Project (SNAP)** dataset at Stanford (http://snap.stanford.edu/data):

1. Start spark-shell with the graphframes package:

```
$ spark-shell --packages graphframes:graphframes:0.2.0-
  spark2.0-s_2.11
```

2. Do the necessary imports:

```scala
scala> import org.graphframes._
```

3. Let's load the road data (tab separated):

```scala
scala> val edges = spark.read.option("delimiter","\t").option
  ("header","true").option("inferschema","true")
    .csv("s3a://sparkcookbook/roads/ca")
```

4. Data is in the format of `(intersection/endpoint intersection/endpoint)`, so to create a `vertex` DataFrame, we need to extract the maximum value of vertex from `edges`:

```scala
scala> val vertices = edges.select("src").union
  (edges.select("dst")).distinct.toDF("id")
```

5. Create a GraphFrame:

```scala
scala> val g = GraphFrame(vertices, edges)
```

6. We think that in California, all roads are connected to each other. Let's see how many connected components there are (it is recommended to be run on DataBricks Cloud or EMR as it would need some heavy duty computations):

```scala
scala> val cc = g.connectedComponents.run
```

7. Let's print the `cc` schema:

```scala
scala> cc.printSchema
root
|-- id: integer (nullable = true)
|-- component: long (nullable = true)
```

8. We are interested in knowing how many connected components there are. So, let's select the `component` column and do the count:

```scala
scala> cc.select("component").distinct.count
(1) Spark Jobs
res7: Long = 2638
```

So, the value comes to `2638`. So in California, every road is not connected with each other, unlike what we would expect. It looks like freeways are not added to this list, and that explains the `2638` clusters.

12
Optimizations and Performance Tuning

This chapter covers various optimization and performance tuning best practices when working with Spark.

The chapter is divided into the following recipes:

- Optimizing memory
- Leveraging speculation
- Optimizing joins
- Using compression to improve performance
- Using serialization to improve performance
- Optimizing level of parallelism
- Understanding project Tungsten

Optimizing memory

Spark is a complex distributed computing framework and has many moving parts. Various cluster resources, such as memory, CPU, and network bandwidth, can become bottlenecks at various points. As Spark is an in-memory compute framework, the impact of the memory is the biggest.

Another issue is that it is common for Spark applications to use a huge amount of memory, sometimes more than 100 GB. This amount of memory usage is not common in traditional Java applications.

In Spark, there are two places where memory optimization is needed: one at the driver level and the other at the executor level. The following diagram shows the two levels (driver level and executor level) of operations in Spark:

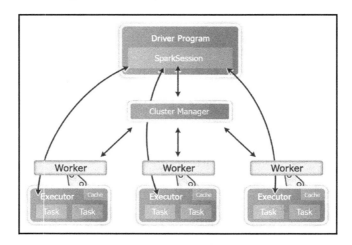

How to do it...

1. Set the driver memory using the `spark-shell` command:

   ```
   $ spark-shell --drive-memory 8g
   ```

2. Set the driver memory using the `spark-submit` command:

   ```
   $ spark-submit --drive-memory 8g
   ```

3. Set the executor memory using the `spark-shell` command:

   ```
   $ spark-shell --executor-memory 8g
   ```

4. Set the executor memory using the `spark-submit` command:

   ```
   $ spark-submit --executor-memory 8g
   ```

5. Sometimes master and worker daemons are starved of memory for their own house-keeping. You can set the daemon memory using the `spark-shell` command:

   ```
   $ spark-shell --daemon-memory 8g
   ```

6. Set the daemon memory using the `spark-submit` command:

```
$ spark-submit --daemon-memory 8g
```

How it works...

Now, the question arises: how do we decide how much executor memory we should allocate? To do this calculation, let's think of a hypothetical cluster with the following nodes:

- 16 nodes
- 16 cores per node
- 256 GB RAM per node

Every node has one worker, each worker has multiple executors, and each executor has multiple tasks as shown in the preceding diagram. So, before deciding how much memory we should allocate to each executor, we have to decide how many executors we would like per core. One extreme can be having one executor per core and allocating 15 GB of RAM per executor. There are two challenges here:

- The system overhead also needs some CPU cycles and memory. So let's give it one core and 16 GB RAM, and that leaves us with 15 cores and 240 GB RAM.
- Every executor has multiple tasks, which share the cached data. If we only assign one executor per core, we are losing the chance to have parallelism in the executor.

How about we go to the other extreme, that is, having one executor per node? The challenge here is the fourth parameter in the cluster, which we have not discussed yet, and that is storage. With one executor, storage parallelism will suffer. So, the best idea is to keep around five cores per executor, and that makes it three executors per node. This gives each executor 80 GB.

Executor memory controls the total heap size, but we need to provision some capacity for off-heap memory, which takes care of things such as **Java Virtual Machine** (**JVM**) overhead, internal strings, and so on. This is controlled by the `spark.yarn.executor.memory.overhead` parameter, and it's default value is 384 MB or 10 percent. So, that brings the `--executor-memory` value to 80/1.1 ~ 72 GB.

Garbage collection

To understand memory optimization, it is a good idea to understand how memory management works in Java. Objects reside in heap in Java. Heap is created when JVM starts, and it can resize itself when needed (based on the minimum and maximum size, that is, –Xms and –Xmx, respectively, assigned in the configuration).

Heap is divided into two spaces or generations: young space and old space, as shown in the following figure:

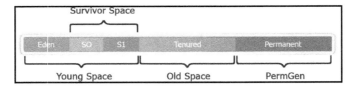

The young space is reserved for the allocation of new objects. The young space consists of an area called **Eden** and two smaller survivor spaces. When the young space becomes full, garbage is collected by running a special process called **young collection**, where all the objects that have lived long enough are promoted to the old space. When the old space becomes full, the garbage is collected there by running a process called **old collection**.

The logic behind nursery/young space is that most objects have a very short lifespan. A young collection is designed to be fast at finding newly allocated objects and moving them to the old space.

Mark and sweep

JVM uses the **mark and sweep** algorithm for garbage collection. Mark and sweep collection consists of two phases.

During the mark phase, all the objects that have live references are marked alive, the rest are presumed candidates for garbage collection. During the sweep phase, the space occupied by the garbage collectable candidates is added to the free list, that is, they are available to be allocated to the new objects.

There are two improvements to mark and sweep. One is **concurrent mark and sweep** (**CMS**), and the other is **parallel mark and sweep**. CMS focuses on lower latency, while the latter focuses on higher throughput. Both strategies have performance trade-offs. CMS does not do compaction, while parallel **garbage collector** (**GC**) performs only whole-heap compaction, which results in pause times. As a thumb rule, for real-time streaming, CMS should be used; parallel GC otherwise.

G1

If you would like to have both low latency and high throughput, Java 1.7 update 4 onwards has another option called garbage-first GC (G1). G1 is a server-style garbage collector, primarily meant for multicore machines with large memories. It is planned as a long-term replacement for CMS. So, to modify our thumb rule, if you are using Java 7 onwards, simply use G1.

G1 partitions the heap into a set of equal-sized regions, where each set is a contiguous range of virtual memory. Each region is assigned a role, such as Eden, Survivor, Old. G1 performs a concurrent global marking phase to determine the live references of objects throughout the heap. After the mark phase is over, G1 knows which regions are mostly empty. It collects objects with no live references, in these regions first, and this frees the larger amount of memory. A typical G1 heap may look like this:

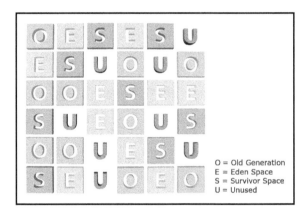

The regions selected by G1 as candidates for garbage collection are garbage collected using evacuation. G1 copies objects from one or more regions of the heap to a single region on the heap, and it both compacts and frees up memory. This evacuation is performed in parallel on multiple cores to reduce pause times and increase throughput. So, each garbage collection round reduces fragmentation while working within user-defined pause times.

There are three aspects in memory optimization in Java:

- Memory footprint
- Cost of accessing objects in memory
- Cost of garbage collection

Java objects, in general, are fast to access but consume much more space than the actual data inside them.

JVM garbage collection can be a challenge if you have a lot of short-lived RDDs. JVM needs to go over all the objects to find the ones it needs to garbage collect. The cost of the garbage collection is proportional to the number of objects the GC needs to go through. Therefore, using fewer objects and the data structures that use fewer objects (simpler data structures, such as arrays) helps.

Serialization also shines here as a byte array needs only one object to be garbage collected.

Spark memory allocation

By default, Spark uses 60 percent of the JVM heap for Spark's execution and storage needs and 40 percent for user objects and metadata. Out of this 60 percentage, 50 percentage of the executor memory is for cache RDDs/DataFrames (storage) and the other 50 percent for execution. Sometimes, you may not need 60 percent for RDDs and can reduce this limit so that more space is available for object creation (and less need for GC).

You can set the memory allocated for the RDD/DataFrame cache to 40 percent by starting the Spark shell and setting the memory fraction:

```
$ spark-shell —conf spark.memory.storageFraction=0.4
```

Spark also has another property, which expresses memory as a fraction to total JVM head space (the default being `0.6`):

```
$ spark-shell —conf spark.memory.fraction=0.7
```

Leveraging speculation

Like MapReduce, Spark uses speculation to spawn additional tasks if it suspects a task is running on a straggler node. A good use case would be to think of a situation when 95 percent or 99 percent of your job finishes really fast and then gets stuck (we have all been there).

How to do it...

There are a few settings you can use to control speculation. The examples are provided only to show how to change values. Mostly, just turning on speculation is good enough:

1. Setting `spark.speculation` (the default is `false`):

```
$ spark-shell —conf spark.speculation=true
```

2. Setting `spark.speculation.interval` (the default is `100` milliseconds) (denotes the rate at which Spark examines tasks to see whether speculation is needed):

   ```
   $ spark-shell —conf spark.speculation.interval=200
   ```

3. Setting `spark.speculation.multiplier` (the default is `1.5`) (denotes how many times a task has to be slower than median to be a candidate for speculation):

   ```
   $ spark-shell —conf spark.speculation.multiplier=1.5
   ```

4. Setting `spark.speculation.quantile` (the default is `0.75`) (denotes the percentage of tasks to be completed before triggering speculation):

   ```
   $ spark-shell —conf spark.speculation.quantile=0.95
   ```

Optimizing joins

This topic was covered briefly when discussing Spark SQL, but it is a good idea to discuss it here again as joins are highly responsible for optimization challenges.

There are primarily three types of joins in Spark:

- Shuffle hash join (default):
    - Classic map-reduce type join
    - Shuffle both datasets based on output key
    - During reduce, join the datasets for same output key
- Broadcast hash join:
    - When one dataset is small enough to fit in memory
- Cartesian join
    - When every row of one table is joined with every row of the other table

The easiest optimization is that if one of the datasets is small enough to fit in memory, it should be broadcast (broadcast join) to every compute node. This use case is very common as data needs to be combined with side data like a dictionary all the time.

Mostly, joins are slow due to too much data being shuffled over the network.

How to do it...

You can also check which execution strategy is being used using `explain`:

```scala
scala> mydf.explain
scala> mydf.queryExecution.executedPlan
```

Using compression to improve performance

Data compression involves encoding information using fewer bits than the original representation. Compression has an important role to play in big data technologies. It makes both storage and transport of data more efficient.

When data is compressed, it becomes smaller, so both disk I/O and network I/O become faster. It also saves storage space. Every optimization has a cost, and the cost of compression comes in the form of added CPU cycles to compress and decompress data.

Hadoop needs to split data to put them into blocks, irrespective of whether the data is compressed or not. Only a few compression formats are splittable.

The two most popular compression formats for big data loads are **Lempel-Ziv-Oberhumer (LZO)** and Snappy. Snappy is not splittable, while LZO is. Snappy, on the other hand, is a much faster format.

If the compression format is splittable like LZO, the input file is first split into blocks and then compressed. Since compression happened at the block level, decompression can happen at the block level as well as the node level.

If the compression format is not splittable, compression happens at the file level, and then it is split into blocks. In this case, blocks have to be merged back to file before they can be decompressed, so decompression cannot happen at the node level.

For supported compression formats, Spark will deploy codecs automatically to decompress, and no action is required from the user's side.

How to do it...

To persist a DataFrame in a specific compression format, all you have to do is to provide compression as an option like this:

```scala
scala>
mydf.write.option("compression","snappy").parquet("hdfs://localhost:9000/us
er/hduser/mydata")
```

Spark also supports `lz4` and `lzf`, besides Snappy.

Using serialization to improve performance

Serialization plays an important part in distributed computing. There are two persistence (storage) levels that support serializing RDDs:

- `MEMORY_ONLY_SER`: This stores RDDs as serialized objects. It will create one byte array per partition.
- `MEMORY_AND_DISK_SER`: This is similar to `MEMORY_ONLY_SER`, but it spills partitions that do not fit in the memory to disk.

How to do it...

The following are the steps to add appropriate persistence levels:

1. Start the Spark shell:

   ```
   $ spark-shell
   ```

2. Import the `StorageLevel` object as enumeration of persistence levels and the implicits associated with it:

   ```scala
   scala> import org.apache.spark.storage.StorageLevel._
   ```

3. Create a dataset:

   ```scala
   scala> val words = spark.read.textFile("words")
   ```

4. Persist the dataset:

   ```scala
   scala> words.persist(MEMORY_ONLY_SER)
   ```

Though serialization reduces the memory footprint substantially, it adds extra CPU cycles due to deserialization.

 By default, Spark uses Java's serialization. Since the Java serialization is slow, the better approach is to use the Kryo library. Kryo is much faster and sometimes even 10 times more compact than the default.

There's more...

You can use Kryo by doing the following settings in your `SparkConf`:

1. Start the Spark shell by setting Kryo as a serializer:

```
$ spark-shell --conf
spark.serializer=org.apache.spark.serializer.KryoSerializer
```

2. Kryo automatically registers most of the core Scala classes, but if you would like to register your own classes, you can use the following command:

```
scala>
sc.getConf.registerKryoClasses(Array(classOf[com.infoobjects.CustomClass1],
classOf[com.infoobjects.CustomClass2])
```

Optimizing the level of parallelism

Optimizing the level of parallelism is very important to fully utilize the cluster capacity. In the case of HDFS, it means that the number of partitions is the same as the number of input splits, which is mostly the same as the number of blocks. The default block size in HDFS is 128 MB, and that works well in case of Spark as well.

In this recipe, we will cover different ways to optimize the number of partitions.

How to do it...

Specify the number of partitions when loading a file into RDD with the following steps:

1. Start the Spark shell:

```
$ spark-shell
```

2. Load the RDD with a custom number of partitions as a second parameter:

```scala
scala> sc.textFile("hdfs://localhost:9000/user/hduser/words",10)
```

Another approach is to change the default parallelism by performing the following steps:

1. Start the Spark shell with the new value of default parallelism:

```
$ spark-shell --conf spark.default.parallelism=10
```

Have the number of partitions two to three times the number of cores to maximize parallelism.

2. Check the default value of parallelism:

```scala
scala> sc.defaultParallelism
```

You can also reduce the number of partitions using an RDD method called `coalesce(numPartitions)`, where `numPartitions` is the final number of partitions you would like. If you want the data to be reshuffled over the network, you can call the RDD method called `repartition(numPartitions)`, where `numPartitions` is the final number of partitions you would like.

Understanding project Tungsten

Project Tungsten, starting with Spark Version 1.4, was the initiative to bring Spark closer to bare metal, which has become a first-class integral feature now. The goal of this project is to substantially improve the memory and CPU efficiency of the Spark applications and push the limits of the underlying hardware.

In distributed systems, conventional wisdom has been to always optimize network I/O as that has been the most scarce and bottlenecked resource. This trend has changed in the last few years. Network bandwidth in the last 5 years has changed from 1 gigabit per second to 10 gigabit per second. In fact, Amazon Web Services is poised to make 40 Gbps standard, and there are already instances available at 20 Gbps.

On similar lines, the disk bandwidth has increased from 50 MB/s to 500 MB/s, and **solid state drives (SSDs)** are being deployed more and more. Pruning unneeded input data and predicate push-down have made the speed gains even larger effectively. Compressed data formats, in the same way, have also helped I/O.

CPU clock speed, on the other hand, was ~3 GHz 5 years back and is still the same. This has unseated the network and made CPU the new bottleneck in distributed processing.

Another trend that has put more load on CPU performance is the new compressed data formats, such as Parquet. Both compression and serialization, as we saw in the previous recipes in this chapter, lead to more CPU cycles. This trend has also pushed the need for CPU optimization to reduce the CPU cycle cost.

On similar lines, let's look at the memory footprint. In Java, GC does memory management. GC has done an amazing job at taking away the memory management from the programmer and making it transparent. To do this, Java has to put a lot of overhead, and that substantially increases the memory footprint. For example, a simple string abcd, which should ideally take 4 bytes, takes 48 bytes in Java.

How to do it...

1. Tungsten is enabled by default, but you can change it using following command:

```
$ spark-shell --conf spark.sql.tungsten.enabled=false
```

2. To re-enable Tungsten use the following command:

```
$ spark-shell --conf spark.sql.tungsten.enabled=true
```

How it works...

Let's understand the evolution of Tungsten in two phases.

Tungsten phase 1

One of the biggest features of Tungsten is to make Java GC irrelevant. Let's look deeper into it.

Bypassing GC

What if we do away with GC and manage memory manually like in lower-level programming languages, such as C? Java does provide a way to do that since version 1.7, and it is called `sun.misc.Unsafe`. Unsafe essentially means that you can build long regions of memory without any safety checks. Utilizing unsafe rows and off-heap memory and doing manual memory management was the first feature of project Tungsten.

Manual memory management by leveraging application semantics, which can be very risky if you do not know what you are doing, is a blessing with Spark. We used our knowledge of data schema (DataFrames) to directly lay out the memory ourselves. It not only gets rid of GC overheads but lets you minimize the memory footprint.

The second point is storing data in CPU cache versus memory. Everyone knows CPU cache is great, as it takes three cycles to get data from the main memory versus one cycle in the cache. This is the second feature of project Tungsten.

Cache conscious computation

Algorithms and data structures are used to exploit memory hierarchy and enable more cache-aware computation.

CPU caches are small pools of memory that store the data the CPU is going to need next. CPUs have two types of caches: instruction cache and data cache. Data caches are arranged in a hierarchy of L1, L2, and L3:

- L1 cache is the fastest and most expensive cache in a computer. It stores the most critical data and is the first place the CPU looks for information.
- L2 cache is slightly slower than L1 but is still located on the same processor chip. It is the second place the CPU looks for information.
- L3 cache is still slower but is shared by all cores, such as **dynamic random-access memory (DRAM)**.

These can be seen in the following diagram:

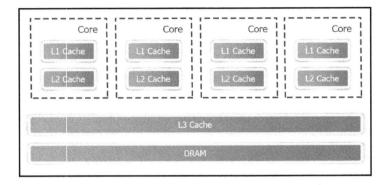

Code generation for expression evaluation

The third point is that Java is not very good at byte code generation for things such as expression evaluation. If this code generation is done manually, it is much more efficient. Code generation is the third feature of project Tungsten.

This involves exploiting modern compliers and CPUs to allow efficient operations directly on binary data. It reduces virtual function calls and interpretation overhead.

Tungsten phase 2

Now let's understand phase 2.

Wholesale code generation

Wholesale code generation essentially does fusing of operators together so that it looks like custom-written code, just to run one single query.

In-memory columnar format

As we saw in the previous chapter, file formats such as Parquet already use the columnar format; the same benefits are being realized with Spark using a columnar format in memory. Some of the benefits are as follows:

- Denser storage
- Compatibility with external already columnar formats, such as Parquet TensorFlow

Index

www.ingramcontent.com/pod-product-compliance
Lightning Source LLC
LaVergne TN
LVHW081337050326
832903LV00024B/1179